HOTEL AND CATERING
CASE STUDIES

Other hotel and catering texts available from the publisher:

HOTEL AND CATERING CASE STUDIES

Peter Abbott
BSc (Hons) Econ, ACIS, AMNIM

Principal Lecturer, Hotel, Catering and Institutional Management Department, Hollings Faculty, Manchester Polytechnic

John Shepherd
BA, FCMA, DipM, DipIAM, CertEd

Principal Lecturer, Hotel, Catering and Institutional Management Department, Hollings Faculty, Manchester Polytechnic

CASSELL

Cassell Educational Limited
Artillery House, Artillery Row,
London, SW1P 1RT

British Library Cataloguing in Publication Data
Abbott, Peter
Hotel and catering case studies.
1. Great Britain. Hotel & catering industries.
Management – case studies
I. Title   II. Shepherd, John
647′.94′068

ISBN 0–304–31632–6

Typeset by Fakenham Photosetting Limited, Fakenham, Norfolk
Printed and bound by Biddles Ltd, Guildford and King's Lynn

CONTENTS

INTRODUCTION

This book contains a collection of case studies intended for students on hotel and catering management courses, from those at BTEC National Diploma, BTEC Higher National and HCIMA Part 'B' to degree and post-graduate levels. They have been developed by the Hotel, Catering and Institutional Management Department at Hollings Faculty, Manchester Polytechnic, on the basis of research and consultancy carried out over a period of years, and have been used successfully on such courses.

Case studies are a means of developing management skills. Originally they were straightforward illustrations of how particular companies coped with specific problems. However, lecturers soon learned to withhold the company's own solution and to ask students what they would have done in the same situation, thus turning what had originally been examples into management problem-solving exercises. This is the form modern case studies usually take, and is the one used here.

The cases are designed to be *integrative*. To get the most out of them, you ought to have some familiarity with the subjects which normally contribute to a hotel and catering management course, such as food, beverage and accommodation operations, marketing, accounts, personnel, law and management itself. The cases themselves supplement rather than replace normal textbooks by giving you practice at *applying* some of the concepts and techniques you have already learned within a realistic management problem-solving context.

The book uses a *graduated* and *sequential* approach. It starts with three relatively short cases designed to introduce you to the basic principles and approach, and then passes on to a sequence of more fully developed 'final year' cases which build on their predecessors.

You will notice that the longer cases display a bias towards north-west England. This does not affect the basic principles involved, and no special knowledge of the region is required. The organiza-

1

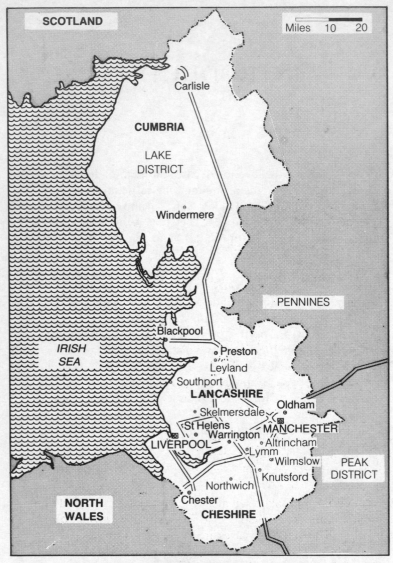

North-west England, showing towns and locations mentioned in the text and main motorway connections.

tions described are fictionalized composites, and no resemblance to any genuine individual or firm is intended.

You will also notice that the events described in the major cases are all dated squarely in the mid-1980s. This is because we wanted to link some of them together (though they can of course be used as self-contained cases as well). We selected 1985 as a common closing date in order to ensure consistency of data. Again, this does not affect the basic principles involved, since it is usually the trends revealed by the comparative figures which are important, rather than the figures themselves.

Eventually, of course, any case study will be rendered obsolete by technological or social developments (an eighteenth-century hotel case, for instance, might have concerned itself with stabling for the guests' horses and accommodation for his servants). We trust this won't happen to ours *too* rapidly! However, even if changes do occur, many establishments (particularly the smaller and more old-fashioned ones) would retain the older system for several years, and you could treat the ones described in our cases as typical of those. In such circumstances we would expect your answer to include an evaluation of the new system and a comparison in terms of costs and efficiency with the old.

Finally, you may notice that some of the proposals in the longer cases are not 'worked through' as they would be in real life. This is deliberate, if a little unrealistic. The best way to think of them is as preliminary drafts which it is your job to complete. We have tried to present you with enough information to do this yourselves.

HOW TO USE THIS BOOK

Like all exercises, these case studies are intended to be *worked through*. That way you will be practising the skills of analysis and problem-solving instead of just reading about them. Approach the cases in this way and you will have made a sensible management decision at the very outset!

The sequential approach used means that the later cases build on their predecessors. This means that you ought to work through them in order. The first three cases are intended to introduce you to some of the principles involved. The next five are broadly of the same standard and are equally suitable for degree, postgraduate or final year BTEC students. The last case raises strategic issues and is consequently set at a rather higher level.

The cases can be tackled on either an individual or a syndicate basis. There is a lot to be said for the latter approach. After all, they were prepared on a collaborative basis, and it makes sense to answer them in the same way. A syndicate can generate more ideas than an individual, as well as subjecting them to a more critical review. Moreover, the process develops qualities such as teamwork and oral communication which our educational system has been accused of neglecting.

In the same way, answers can be presented on either a group or an individual basis. Either way, however, we would urge that the presentation should include a formal written report. The cases themselves are quite lengthy and detailed, and an oral response based on a single reading is likely to be too superficial to be of any value.

The instructions can be varied to suit the level required. If you are a relatively advanced student, we suggest a very 'open' formula along the following lines:

'Analyse the current situation and submit your recommendations regarding future policy.'

This allows you to decide what the problems are for yourself, just as a real manager would have to do. However, we recognize that case studies can be rather formidable things to tackle, and so we have added a number of suggestions as to how each might be approached. These suggestions are not intended to cover every possible point, and you may well find additional issues which are worth exploring.

We have included outline 'answers' for the first three introductory case studies. You will find these in the Appendix at the back.

ANSWERING CASE STUDIES

How do you go about answering a case study? The best way to learn this is to work through the cases in the book, but some introductory points may be helpful.

Since case studies are management problem-solving exercises, you should try to use the classic problem-solving approach, which can be summarized as follows:

1. Establish the facts.

2. Analyse those facts and draw appropriate conclusions.

3. Define the problem or problems.

4. List your alternative courses of action, with pros and cons for each.

5. Make appropriate recommendations, including proposals for implementation.

This format should not be applied rigidly to every case study, especially since many will require an answer structured along specific lines, but its ideas should underline your approach throughout. Let us look at these steps in a little more detail.

Establishing the Facts

The facts are presented in the case. Unfortunately, there may well be rather a lot of them, since case studies tend to be much longer than single subject problems. There are of course 'one page' cases designed to form part of a conventional unseen examination paper, but the true business school case may very well cover fifty pages or more. Though daunting, this is inevitable, because management problems are necessarily complex, often involving the balancing of technical, financial and social considerations, and they are hard to simplify because the interplay of these factors is an essential part of the problem.

Some of the details provided may appear to be more relevant than others. With the smaller, 'one page' type of case study you can usually assume that *all* the information supplied is relevant in some way or other, if only because the writer has had to compress a complex situation into a very limited space, and has been forced to select the material carefully. This ceases to be true as case studies get larger. After all, real life tends to be full of distractions, and one of a manager's problems is to avoid being sidetracked. It would be quite legitimate for case study writers to include extraneous material and even deliberate 'red herrings' in order to test your ability to recognize and keep to the main point. On the whole, however, this right is used sparingly, and you will generally find that even apparently irrelevant 'anecdotal' information helps to give you an idea of the general feel of the operation. After all, in real life, managers do not restrict themselves to reports and accounts: they get out and about, talking to customers and staff in an attempt to assess intangibles like mood and atmosphere.

Even so, you may feel that a case doesn't provide you with anything like *enough* information. This could well be true by absolute standards, but you must remember that real-life managers often feel they don't have enough information either, often because it would cost too much in terms of time or money to collect. All a manager can do in such circumstances is to try to make some reasonable assumptions about the present situation, and then resolve to change the record-keeping system so that it provides the necessary information in the future (indeed, a recommendation along these lines might very well be part of the 'answer' to a case study). On the whole, the facts you are given ought to be those available to a real-life manager in an equivalent situation. As we've already said, you can't expect to know *everything*.

In principle, you should restrict yourself to the facts given in the case study. This doesn't mean that you can't use general background knowledge, but don't do so if this conflicts with information specifically presented in the case. In one or two instances, for example, we have deliberately simplified the competitive position in real-life towns like Chester or Knutsford. If you know these places you may feel inclined to add points we have left out. Please don't. In a sense, our 'Chester' and our 'Knutsford' are imaginary creations which happen to have the same names as the real ones.

The most important thing to remember is that you should *use* the facts in your answer instead of just *repeating* them. You may find that it helps you to begin your answer with a brief summary, but there really isn't much point in regurgitating case material by itself without any kind of comment.

Drawing Conclusions

This is an important part of the process of analysis. Raw data can often be made to yield a good deal of significant information (a simple illustration of this is when raw figures are turned into percentages), and you should try out whatever techniques you may have been taught. Don't try to be too sophisticated, however: your main tool ought to be ordinary common sense.

This is particularly true when you are making assumptions about people's motives and behaviour. It is tempting to invent very elaborate conspiracies assuming all kinds of possible (but unlikely) relationships, but the ordinary, dull, common-sense explanation which involves the fewest assumptions is by far the best (this principle was first articulated by William of Occam back in the fourteenth century, and it hasn't really been improved on since).

You are entitled to assume that any information you are given is factual and correct (errors and omissions always excepted, of course), but be careful! If the case says, directly and unambiguously 'The restaurant's meals are of high quality' then that's a fact. If it says 'McGregor, the Restaurant Manager, believes that the restaurant serves high-quality meals' then it's a fact that McGregor believes this but it isn't necessarily true that the meals are as good as he thinks. If complaints were high and repeat business down you ought to query his standards. In other words, you need to read between the lines. This has its real-life parallel too: it is often what people *don't* say that tells you most.

Diagnosing the Problems

This is one of the trickiest and most important stages of all, and it will help if you have a clear idea of what you are trying to achieve. The key is to approach the problem from a *management* point of view. Managers are responsible for co-ordinating the activities of a number of other people (some being subordinates, others colleagues, outside suppliers or even superiors) in order to achieve the organization's objectives as efficiently as possible. In a case study, as in real life, these objectives are usually implied or 'understood' rather than stated explicitly, but if they differ from the normal commercial objective of long-term survival you are entitled to have this made clear.

This 'management' perspective means that problems may have more than one dimension. For example, you could be faced with a disciplinary situation which might give grounds for summary dismissal. Deciding whether it does or not is a *legal* problem: deciding whether to take that course, with all its possible repercussions in terms of possible appeals and its effect on staff morale, is a *management* problem. Another example is where you have two equivalent problems on your desk at the same time, one perhaps financial, the other technical. Both require solutions, but there's a third management problem involved as well, namely which should you tackle first?

It might help you to think in terms of symptoms and fundamental causes. The accounts may reveal weaknesses in terms of falling sales, or rising costs, or both. These are problems, but you need to trace them back to their origins, which may lie in the organization's marketing policy, or its manpower policy, or (again) both. Alternatively, you might think in terms of both short-term and long-term problems. A deficiency in working capital has to be remedied pretty quickly, otherwise the business will go bust, but an injection of new capital won't do much good in the long term unless it is accompanied by policy changes designed to make sure that the same situation won't occur again in a few months' time. Indeed, you'll find it hard to convince anyone to let you have more capital unless you can convince them that you can improve the operation.

Make sure that you have not only identified the problems but listed them as well. If you don't do this, you might find yourself skipping over them when you come to your recommendations. Write them down, so that later on you can come back and check on whether the course of action you propose to take will actually solve the problems.

Identifying Alternative Courses of Action

Your next step is to consider the various options open to you and their likely consequences. This is another important step, so treat it seriously and try to make your list as complete as possible.

One course of action would be to do nothing. As many managers will testify, this often works in real life, and you should consider it if only because working out the consequences of inaction will help you to appreciate the need to do *something*. It may seem obvious, but it isn't a waste of time to write 'If I do nothing, the problems I've identified aren't likely to get any better: in fact they'll probably get worse, perhaps because the staff will conclude that I am weak and ineffective . . .'

The earlier analysis and diagnosis stages of most case studies are relatively straightforward, and it is at this point that imagination and creativity come into their own. The more alternatives you can think of, the more choice you will have, and the better your eventual answer is likely to be. Sometimes the best answer of all turns out to be one that the writers hadn't thought of!

Recommendations

Managers have to make decisions, and so, in a case study situation, do you. It is very tempting to respond 'I would try to carry out an extensive investigation before making up my mind', but, as we have said, this is often not possible in real life. It is also tempting, when faced with a difficult problem, to say, 'I would refer this to head office for instructions'. In real life you probably would, but good managers would still add their own recommendations, and in a case study situation you are both the manager on-the-spot *and* the head office. In other words, you can't evade responsibility. Case studies are a means of developing management skills, and one of the most important of these is decision-making.

Needless to say, you ought to give your reasons for making any recommendations. Normally these should relate back to the problems you have identified (which is why it is necessary you list these). There could well be some overlap between this and the preceding section inasmuch as you may already have listed your final recommendation as one of the alternative courses of action and detailed the likely consequences. This is very much a problem of composition.

Avoid the 'shotgun' approach. Quite often, answers say in effect 'I would increase sales by spending more on marketing and appealing to the young, the middle-aged and the elderly, male and female, married and unmarried. At the same time I would decrease costs, improve staff morale and carry out a thorough programme of re-equipment and redecoration . . .' Quite so. Unfortunately, there is usually only so much cash in the kitty, and a product designed to appeal to one market segment will not necessarily appeal to another. In other words, it is important that you produce a set of recommendations that are both realistic and consistent.

This leads us on to the question of implementation. A good case study answer not only indicates *what* ought to be done, but spells out *how* it should be done, *when* it should be done (and, if there are several things, in what order), *how much* it is all likely to cost, *where* the money could come from, and, finally, *who* ought to take responsibility. Obviously, you can't be expected to produce detailed blueprints, but outline or skeleton plans, costings, schedules and projections will improve your answer immensely.

Presentation

If decision-making is one of the two great management skills, communication is the other, and you will benefit enormously if you try to practise communicating as a manager. You may well be tempted to jot down your analysis in the form of rough notes. This is all very well, but remember that rough notes wouldn't be acceptable to head office, and we hope you will take time and trouble over your answer. Whatever you do, you *must* avoid the trap of producing an essay. Essays are all very well in their place, but managers don't write essays: they write *reports*. Therefore, you must practise report-style presentation.

This is not the place to go into report writing in detail. Any good library will contain a number of excellent books on the subject. All we will say is that you should use common sense about what features you need to adopt in your answer. Headings and subheadings are essential, since they help you to think systematically about how your material is to be organized, but you don't really need to number your paragraphs since this is chiefly designed to help committees find their way around long and complex documents. Putting a summary and conclusions at the front is good practice in real life, but it's awkward to manage in what is really an exercise. If you think of your answer as a draft for typing, and concentrate on the basic structure rather than the trimmings, you shouldn't go far wrong. Keep it clear, keep it simple, and avoid flippancy and anything that smacks of fine writing. It may sound dull, but your model ought to be the better sort of civil service prose.

Finally, you should try to stay within your role. A case study often places you in a specific management position, and you should try to write your report from that standpoint. This can set you some interesting problems. You might, for example, find that you need to criticize some of the policies laid down by the very person you are submitting your report to. This could well happen to you in real life, and it is a useful skill to practise early on (as is explaining away unsatisfactory results).

Finally, a diagrammatic reminder of case study technique is provided.

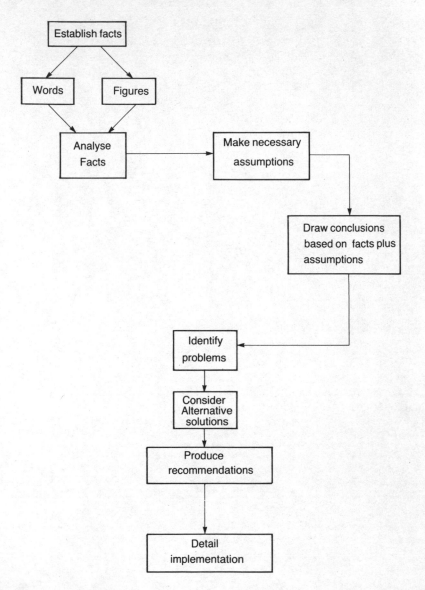

CHAPTER 1

THE DUBBINGTONS CASE

The best way to begin is to attempt an actual case study. This first one is intended as an introductory case. It is therefore quite brief.

CASE STUDY

Chrissie is a relatively new 17-year-old waitress at Dubbingtons, a large department store. One Saturday afternoon store security officers stop her as she is leaving, search her bags and find 11 lb of sliced ham and half-a-dozen eggs in them.

Chrissie admits that these came from the store restaurant's stocks, but claims that she was given them by Fred, the chef, in return for her helping out over her lunch break in the kitchen, which was short handed. Fred denies her story emphatically. 'She's a lying little ****,' he says. 'You know I've no authority to make that sort of deal!'

Fred has been employed at Dubbingtons for the past twelve years. He is a big, genial man of 45, well liked by the other middle-rank departmental staff and undeniably possessed of excellent craft skills. However, the catering department (which comprises the customer restaurant, tea-room, coffee bar and staff canteen) has suffered for several years from higher than average food cost percentages and labour turnover.

The store has recently created the post of Catering Manager to control this side of its operations, and you have been appointed. You have been in the post for three weeks, and this is your second confrontation with Fred. The first was over the board's decision to close the senior staff dining-room and require staff to eat in the staff canteen: Fred apparently thinks you initiated this policy, and resents the fact that he will no longer be able to produce a limited number of high-quality meals and thus ingratiate himself with the senior staff.

There are few records, and those available throw little light on the reasons for the high food costs or the labour turnover in the catering sections. Fred's attitude of surly non-cooperativeness makes further investigation difficult. The other catering staff are non-committal, and it is very unlikely that they will be prepared to 'tell tales' against either Chrissie or Fred.

How would you deal with this situation?

Well, how *should* you? As it happens, this is one of those cases where you can use the classic problem-solving approach more or less as it stands.

The first thing to do is to re-read the case thoroughly until you are confident that you have assimilated all the facts (this isn't too difficult with a short case like this one, but is a bit harder with the longer ones). Some students find that it helps them to make a brief précis of the situation, though you shouldn't waste too much time in writing out points which you already have set down in front of you.

The second stage is to see what conclusions you can draw from the facts: in other words, to try to fit these into a pattern that makes sense. What has really been going on in this establishment? The facts – that Chrissie has been caught taking food home, the higher than average food costs, etc. – show that things haven't been going entirely according to plan, but what are the *causes*? Answering this kind of question will inevitably involve you in a certain amount of guesswork, because you can't know for certain what has been going on, but some assumptions are more likely than others. For instance, there is a whole range of factors which *could* lead to high food costs, including bad purchasing, storage or portion control, but there isn't any supporting evidence in the case itself for most of these. On the other hand, there *is* some supporting evidence for an explanation based on pilferage. Ask yourself whether the other facts are consistent with this explanation, and see whether you can come up with a pattern of events which makes sense in terms of ordinary human nature.

The next stage is to identify the problems. As we have already said, make sure that you list them as well. Don't make the mistake of concentrating just on the *immediate* problem. This is a well-known pitfall in real life as well as in case studies. Keep in mind that your real objective is to get this unit running smoothly and efficiently.

Next, you have to consider the options open to you and their likely consequences. Remember that one of these options is to do nothing, though you may well feel that this is one of those cases where this course of action (or *in*action) would simply make matters worse. Clearly, you have to make up your mind what to do about Chrissie, and you should also think hard about Fred, the chef. Be careful, though. It's no good writing something down as an option unless you actually have the power to do it. And be realistic. It isn't much good writing 'I would carry out a thorough investigation and get to the bottom of this whole business . . .' The case has already given you Fred's answer, and what you are told about Fred suggests (deliberately) that he is a pretty tough, hard-bitten sort of character. How likely is it that he would change his story? The case has already told you that the records are incomplete. How likely is it that the other staff would volunteer information, especially about practices in which they themselves might have been involved?

Once you have established what your options are, you should go on to produce a specific recommendation or set of recommendations. Try to make these *positive*, and if possible try to manage with the resources already available to you. It is tempting to write 'If I had my way, I'd fire all the staff and start all over again', but top management doesn't usually look very kindly on this kind of approach. One of your problems in this case is Fred, the chef: no doubt you would like to see him replaced by someone else who is equally skilled but a lot easier to work with. However, you will get more credit if you can put forward a solution which allows you to operate effectively with the staff you already have. Try to make your recommendations *practical*. If you decide (as you might) that part of the answer lies in changing the system within which the staff are working, then you should outline what changes you propose to make and how you would introduce them to staff, both present and future.

Finally, a word about presentation. We have already indicated that this case can be answered along the classic problem-solving lines, which gives you a ready-made structure for your answer. How long should it be? Well, as a very, *very* rough approximation, you ought to be able to get 3–4 pages of answer out of every page of case study text. This probably sounds horrifying, but once you start, you'll find it very difficult to answer this one adequately in under 3–4 sides. Remember that the facts are only the starting point: you will have a number of assumptions to justify and several courses of action to consider before you submit your final recommendation. Obviously, this last stage shouldn't involve too much repetition: if you've already identified the reasons why this is the best course of action you don't have to repeat them all over again. However, you *could* usefully add some details as to how you would implement your proposal.

You will find an outline 'answer' to this introductory case in the Appendix at the back of the book. However, we do advise you, very strongly, to try it yourself first. As we have said, you can only develop a skill by practising it.

CHAPTER 2

THE HARDY HALL CASE

If you are working through this book in a systematic manner, you will already have attempted the Dubbingtons case and compared your response with our suggested 'answer' at the back of the book. Quite probably you will have discovered that you put much more emphasis than we did on the immediate problem of trying to discover whether it was Chrissie or Fred who was telling the truth. This is a very common response, and it's nothing to worry about as long as you realize that the *manager*'s emphasis has to be on getting the unit to run efficiently. This might well involve getting to the bottom of disputes and taking disciplinary action if necessary, but never forget your real aim is to keep things running.

However, this often involves managers in taking decisions about future policy, and management level case studies commonly invite you to consider whether a change of direction is necessary, and if so, what the operational implications are. Our second introductory case places you in this situation.

CASE STUDY

You are the Domestic Bursar of Hardy Hall, a hall of residence for Casterbridge Polytechnic. You are responsible for the day-to-day running of the hall, including cleaning and catering.

The Hall is situated approximately 5 miles from the Polytechnic in an attractive high income suburb. Originally a large Victorian house set in its own extensive grounds, it was converted in the 1960s into a hall of residence by the addition of a three-storey extension. The main building has a dining-room, kitchen, TV-lounge and reading-room on the ground floor, and a lecture theatre, two seminar rooms, bursar's flat and two toilets on the first floor. The extension has 35 single study-bedrooms, 1 linen room and 3 bathrooms, WCs and utility rooms (one on each floor).

Students are allocated accommodation on a yearly basis, though payment is by termly instalments. They pay a standard £31.50 per week for accommodation and meals as detailed below. In principle, the Hall is occupied for the full academic year of 36 weeks. In practice, student occupancy for the last week of the Christmas and Easter terms averages 50 per cent, while that for the last two weeks of the summer term is 33 per cent.

The staff comprise the following:

- *Yourself (Domestic Bursar).* This is a live-in post with a flat on the first floor. You are responsible for the day-to-day running of the Hall, including overall control of cleaning and catering. Your salary is £8,250 exclusive of live-in benefits, which may be assumed to be equivalent to a further 20 per cent.

- *Tom Gutteridge (Porter/Cleaner).* Responsible for heavy cleaning work, the movement of stores and for odd maintenance jobs (e.g. the replacement of light bulbs etc.), major maintenance being carried out by the Polytechnic's Building Division. He works a normal 8 hour day and is paid at £2.80 per hour.

- *Cleaners.* There are 4 of these. They are employed 7–11 a.m. only. They are paid at £2.36 per hour. All are married women with their own family commitments at weekends.

- *Agnes McCabe (Cook/Kitchen Supervisor).* She is responsible for menu planning and food preparation, though you do the actual purchasing. She works 11 a.m.–7 p.m. and receives a salary of £6,150.

- *Rita Lowndes (Assistant Cook).* Acts as relief to Mrs McCabe and normally covers breakfasts. She works a variable 8 hour day (normally on a split shift basis) and receives £87.50 per week.

- *Two Catering Assistants.* These work split shifts (7–10 a.m., 4–7 p.m.) to cover breakfasts and evening meals and are paid £2.65 per hour.

'Permanent' staff (yourself, the Cook/Kitchen Supervisor and Assistant Cook) are full time. Other staff are laid off during holidays, except that they also work reduced hours (approximately 50 per cent of the term-time totals) for the last two weeks of July (usually weeks 37–38 of the academic year). Staff normally work Monday to Friday only. Daily and weekly paid staff are entitled to receive time-and-a-half for Saturdays and double-time for Sunday and Bank Holiday work. All rates of pay quoted can be assumed to be gross, i.e. inclusive of employer's contributions etc.

Other expenses are as follows:

	£
General rates	2,500
Water rates	500
Lighting and heating	2,400
Repairs and maintenance	2,350
Telephone	400
Sundries	250

Student bedroom heating is normally switched off during holiday periods and that for communal areas reduced to a minimum, but no detailed apportionment has been carried out. Outgoing student calls are made from a pay phone, so that the telephone charge can be regarded as a purely administrative expense.

The catering facilities were changed to cafeteria style service with standard menus and limited choice in 1981 in order to reduce costs. Breakfasts and evening meals are provided Monday to Friday only, the students being expected to obtain their own midday and week-end meals at the Polytechnic or elsewhere. Limited cooking and food storage facilities are, however, available in the utility rooms on each floor. A cooked breakfast is available and is chosen by approximately 75 per cent of resident students: the food cost averages £1.10p. The evening meal generally includes two courses: the food cost averages £1.35p. The premises are not licensed.

It was decided in 1983 that students would in future be required to provide their own bed linen and towels. The Hall's own linen was sold and the proceeds used to purchase coin operated laundry facilities which were situated in the second floor utility room. A linen hire company will collect/deliver laundry every Tuesday and Thursday. The cost of hire is as follows:

Sheet	40p
Pillowcase	18p
Towel	32p

You estimate approximate cleaning times as follows:

Room clean after student departure	45 minutes
Daily clean of bedroom	10 minutes
Room clean after conference departure	20 minutes
Toilet area (daily)	10 minutes

Corridor/stairs per floor (daily)	10 minutes
Communal areas (per area)	
Heavy usage	20 minutes
Light usage	5 minutes

The Polytechnic has recently taken the decision to enter the conference market during vacations and the standard of furnishings, fittings and facilities has been improved with a view to attracting this type of business. However, no policy decisions have been taken regarding the pricing of conferences.

Two conference enquiries have been received with regard to the forthcoming Easter Vacation. The students have already been notified that they will be required to leave by 10 a.m. on Friday 28 March and will return on Saturday 19 April. Details of the applications are attached.

Conference 1: Serendipity for Senior Citizens

Organizers: The Creative Retirement Association

No: 30 participants

Programme:

March		
Fri. 28	3 p.m.	Arrival
	6 p.m.	Dinner
Sat.–Thu.	8.30–9 a.m.	Breakfast
	9.30 a.m.–4.30 p.m.	Local tours/visits (Packed lunch to be provided)
	6 p.m.	Dinner
April		
Fri. 3	8.30–9 a.m.	Breakfast
	10 a.m.	Departure

Notes: All members of this group can be expected to be aged 60 or more and approximately 66 per cent female. No evening functions are planned and no request has been made for licensed facilities.

Conference 2: Case Study Writing for Lecturers

Organizers: The Case Study Research Association

No: 33 participants

Programme:

April

Fri. 3	3 p.m.	Arrival
	5 p.m.	Sherry reception and course introduction in TV lounge
	6 p.m.	Dinner
	7.30–9.30 p.m.	Lectures
Sat. 4	8–8.30 a.m.	Breakfast
	9 a.m.	Lecture
	10.30 a.m.	Coffee and biscuits
	11 a.m.–12.30 p.m.	Seminars (4 groups)
	1 p.m.	Lunch
	2 p.m.	Lecture
	3 p.m.	Tea and biscuits
	3.30–4.30 p.m.	Lecture
	5 p.m.	Sherry reception in TV lounge
	6.30 p.m.	Dinner followed by entertainments in TV lounge/reading room
Sun. 5	8.30–9 a.m.	Breakfast
	9.30 a.m.	Seminars (4 groups)
	11 a.m.	Coffee and biscuits
	11.30 a.m.	Lecture
	1.30 p.m.	Lunch and departure

Notes: Participants can be expected to be in age range 25–55, and approximately 75 per cent male.

You are required to produce a report for the Director of Casterbridge Polytechnic:

1. Detailing the operational implications of the proposed conference bookings.

2. Outlining your proposals regarding the basis to be adopted for conference pricing in general, and recommending specific prices for the two conferences under consideration.

███████████████████████████████████

Since this is another introductory case, a few pointers might be helpful. Dubbingtons was a supervisory problem. In other words, it put you in a relatively junior position and asked you to solve a problem which was relatively limited in scope. This case asks you to consider rather more factors, including the policy to be adopted towards conference bookings and pricing in the future. You have to decide whether you can accommodate either or both of these groups (is there enough time to clean and change the rooms between departure and arrival, for instance?), and what kind of staffing and other arrangements you need to make to cope with them. This isn't just a 'one-off' problem, either, because you are specifically told that the Polytechnic has decided to enter the conference market. In other words, you have to assume that these kind of arrangements will become a permanent feature.

You will also see that the case introduces figures, both financial and statistical. These tend to be looked upon with horror by many students, but you can't expect to deal with any but the simplest management problem without considering them. In fact, it is fairly obvious what you are supposed to do with the ones here. Once you have decided what the extra staffing and other requirements are in respect of the two conferences, you can work out how much it is going to cost to accommodate them. Obviously, you will want to make a profit, but how much? This is a matter of judgement. What we would expect you to do is to consider various alternative methods of pricing and to come out with a recommendation. Remember, the one thing you can't do is duck the issue.

However, there is an important bit of information which is missing, and that is the price being charged by the competition (perhaps a nearby university). In normal circumstances you would know this or be able to find it out, but this is still only a short case study and we haven't included it. The best way to deal with the problem is to make your recommendation and add some such wording as 'subject to modification in the light of the competitive situation'.

You will probably find that you can't lay out your answer along the classic problem-solving lines (Facts–Assumptions–Problems–Alternatives–Recommendations). This doesn't matter, because it will still underlie your response. You will have to make assumptions (for instance, will my regular staff be willing to work holiday weekends?), identify problems (can the cafeteria cope with the rather different demands of the delegates?), and consider alternatives (like the various pricing approaches already mentioned). Finally, you must offer some positive recommendations.

You will find an outline 'answer' to this case in the Appendix at the back of the book. As before, however, we advise you to try it yourself first.

CHAPTER 3

THE CASE OF GEORGE AND MARIE

The Hardy Hall case was both longer than Dubbingtons and couched at a higher level. You had to think about the changes you needed to make to your operation, and you had to support your recommendations with some detailed calculations. The next case might appear to be a bit shorter, but in fact it asks you to consider rather more factors, over a longer period, and from a rather higher management level.

CASE STUDY

George and Marie started L'Auberge, a quality French restaurant, in Chelmslow, a prosperous dormitory village some 15 miles outside Melcaster, the centre of a large metropolitan conurbation. The fact that the restaurant was successful was due largely to the way in which their respective talents complemented each other. Marie originally did most of the cooking, and subsequently continued to supervise menu planning and food purchasing as well as handling the accounting aspects. George's particular talents lay in the field of personal relations. He took most of the responsibility for the selection and training of staff, with whom he enjoyed good relations, and was an excellent host, with a particular knowledge of French wines. L'Auberge maintained an unusually extensive and well-selected wine list, and George was usually on hand to supervise the restaurant and offer advice to customers on the selection of food and drink.

L'Auberge expanded, necessitating the employment of Arnold, a young chef who took over most of the day-to-day running of the kitchen, and Olive, a restaurant manageress who, like almost all the waitresses, lived locally and had been trained on the job by George.

The £30,000 capital with which George and Marie had started in business had now grown to £140,000.

By 1983 the restaurant was averaging 100 covers a day, with a staff of:

Kitchen	Restaurant	Bar
Chef (Arnold)	Manageress (Olive)	Barman (Steve)
2 commis chefs	Cashier	Part-time barman
1 kitchen woman	3 full-time waitresses	
	2 part-time waitresses	

At this point, George and Marie decide to expand by opening a new restaurant in Melcaster itself. Called the Brasserie, it opened on 1 January 1984. The investment of £60,000 was financed 50 per cent from accumulated profits and 50 per cent by a bank loan. It was launched on similar lines to L'Auberge, and with the same staffing structure. Arnold, who had been growing increasingly restive under Marie's close supervision, transferred willingly to the Brasserie, but Olive and the other waitresses refused to leave Chelmslow. Experienced bar and kitchen staff were recruited fairly easily in Melcaster, but it proved difficult to find restaurant staff of the same calibre.

George and Marie agreed that George should take most of the responsibility for the Brasserie, which they felt needed his talent for hospitality to build up a clientele, as well as his ability to train staff and foster good employee relations. Marie remained at L'Auberge because she felt that although Norman, the new chef, was qualified and experienced, he needed to be shown her way of doing things. The immediate result of George's absence was the loss of his advice regarding the wine list, about which Olive knew little, and after three months Marie found it necessary to engage a specialist wine waiter.

The results are shown in the following operating statements:

Year ended:	31/12/83		31/12/84		31/12/85	
	£	£	£	£	£	£
Food sales	180,763		294,434		290,976	
Cost of sales	73,800		126,568		130,369	
Gross profit		106,963		167,866		160,607
Beverage sales	91,050		150,999		152,683	
Cost of sales	39,152		66,440		68,707	
Gross profit		51,898		84,559		83,976
Total gross profit		158,861		252,425		244,583
Labour cost	73,800		154,980		162,360	
Overhead cost	45,000		94,500		99,000	
		118,800		249,480		261,360
Net profit		40,061		2,945		−16,777

24

The Brasserie, which they had hoped would equal L'Auberge's trade, has only averaged 60 covers per day, and L'Auberge itself has fallen off from 90 in 1984 to 75 in 1985. Food costs appear to have risen at both establishments, even though Marie has secured improved terms from the suppliers. George and Marie are very disappointed, especially as they have both been working around the clock since the expansion, managing the Brasserie and L'Auberge respectively, interviewing and training new staff (labour turnover has been high at the Brasserie from the start and is now significantly higher at L'Auberge too) and filling in whenever necessary at either establishment. They both do a considerable amount of travelling, since Marie likes to check the Brasserie's takings and George doesn't want to lose touch with L'Auberge's customers, and this adds to their fatigue. It is obvious that things cannot go on as they are.

What do you think are the reasons for the problems facing George and Marie, and what advice would you give them?

Note: National changes in costs/prices for the period in question were as follows:

	1983 (%)	1984 (%)	1985 (%)
Restaurant prices:	100	106	112
Food costs:	100	102	106
Labour costs:	100	108	113

Since this is yet another introductory case, a few more pointers might be helpful. As we have said, Dubbingtons was a supervisory problem. Hardy Hall put you in a rather higher position and invited you to consider some of the long-term implications of the proposed change as well as the immediate problems. However, it didn't invite you to consider whether that change was sensible or not, and the bulk of it was still concerned with matters of detail. In reality, of course, this is the kind of thing most managers find themselves dealing with for most of the time, especially those in relatively junior positions within large organizations. However, senior managers have to consider where the business as a whole is going, and this kind of problem also has to be faced by anyone trying to run their own business, no matter how small.

We have already said that case studies are 'interdisciplinary', and you will have noticed that even Dubbingtons expected you to use knowledge from at least two different areas (in that instance, law and food and beverage control), while Hardy Hall involved more (finance, personnel, food and beverage and accommodation operations). George and Marie calls for concepts and techniques from an even greater range of disciplines, especially management.

Your main problem is likely to be how to structure (i.e. lay out) your answer. As a general rule, you should find that the actual 'question' offers a useful starting point. In this instance, it asks you to explain what you think are the reasons for the problems facing George and Marie, and then to 'advise' them (in other words, to put forward your own recommendations). This probably calls for a basic two-part structure, with part one detailing your assumptions, deductions and conclusions, and giving your analysis of the problems, while part two looks at possible alternative courses of action and spells out your 'solution'.

This approach is based on the classic problem-solving sequence, but it doesn't mean that your answer has to follow that in every detail. This case is rather more complex than either Dubbingtons or Hardy Hall, and you probably need to use a more structured approach within the sections. One fairly obvious approach is the 'functional' one. You should be familiar with the main 'functional' areas of management: marketing (customer policy), finance (broadly, the accounts) and personnel (staff). Clearly, each such area ought to be able to make some contribution to analysing George and Marie's problems.

Let us take finance as an example. Again, the case introduces figures, both financial and statistical. Obviously, you are expected to 'use' them somehow, but what you are supposed to do with them is rather less obvious than it was in the Hardy Hall case. Hopefully, you already have your own ideas, but if you haven't, you might start by attempting a rough calculation of the average spend per customer. You already know how many covers each restaurant serves per day. The case doesn't actually tell you how many days per week each is open, but a reasonable guess would be six. The case doesn't tell you how many weeks per year each restaurant is open, either, but you can make a reasonable guess about that, too. If you do this calculation for each year, you should find something worth commenting on. Whether what you find wholly explains the overall fall in trade is questionable, but at least it gives you a start.

You can do the same sort of thing with the 'personnel' information, though here you have to make rather more assumptions. Be careful, however. It is very easy to get involved in discussing whether Olive ought to have been given some knowledge of French wines before George moved, or perhaps persuaded to move to the city along with him. These questions should have been foreseen, certainly, but the real personnel issues have more to do with selection, induction and training in general, and the question is whether George's relatively informal system is really suited to the new circumstances. In other words, don't get too bogged down discussing individual personalities (with the possible exception of the joint owner-managers, of course).

The trouble with the 'functional' approach, however, is that it carries with it the risk that you will omit general considerations such as overall objectives and strategy. These tend to be 'hidden' issues in many case studies, and it might be worth seeing whether your points could be covered within a structure based on the management process. There are various alternative renderings of this in different textbooks, but the simplest is as follows:

- Planning

- Organizing

- Motivating

- Controlling.

Clearly, 'planning' (to take just one aspect) ought to cover marketing, financial and personnel considerations, but it also brings in general management as well. This includes not only the co-ordination of the 'functional' plans but the whole nature of the planning process itself. You can probably find things to say about how well George and Marie have gone about co-ordinating their marketing, financial and personnel activities, and you could even ask yourself whether they might not have been wiser to expand (if that is what they still want to do) in a different direction altogether. This is a perfectly valid question to raise in a case study response, and you might go on to consider whether it is still possible for them to change direction, even now.

You will find another outline 'answer' in the Appendix at the back of the book. Once again, however, we advise you to try it yourself first.

CHAPTER 4

THE ROYAL OAK CASE

The Hardy Hall and George and Marie cases introduced you to the idea that case studies ought to include a certain amount of financial and statistical data. In real life, of course, you would probably have to master a great deal more information, including details of the premises and the personal particulars of all the key staff. The next case attempts to introduce you to some of these complexities.

As you will see, the case is about one particular unit. It happens to be part of a small chain of hotels, but you can ignore the broader aspects of the company's activities for the purposes of this particular case and treat it simply as a problem in unit management. We shall be returning to Acorn Hotels Ltd later, however.

You will see that we have located the hotel in Knutsford, which is a real town. The demographic data we have provided are accurate enough, but no resemblance to any existing hotel or hotels in Knutsford is intended, and the competitive position described here is not the same as it is in reality.

CASE STUDY

INTRODUCTION

The Royal Oak is one of four hotels owned and operated by Acorn Hotels Ltd. They are:

Royal Oak, Knutsford	54 rooms, built 1895, purchased 1955
Granville, Northwich	40 rooms, built 1924, purchased 1966
Beechwood, Skelmersdale	36 rooms, built 1937, purchased 1972
Rowan, Leyland	32 rooms, built 1912, purchased 1976

Acorn's policy has been to buy up sound but somewhat shabby family-owned hotels as and when opportunity offers, and to renovate them to an extent consistent with the company's 'image' of old-fashioned comfort.

Acorn is a limited company formed in 1955. Until recently it was run jointly by Peter Davenport and his elder brother Quentin, an accountant by training who supervised the company as a whole while Peter ran the Royal Oak. Quentin Davenport died suddenly in April 1985, and Peter inherited his shares. As a result, 65 per cent of the shares are currently controlled by Peter Davenport and his wife.

Davenport continues to run the Royal Oak, while the other hotels are run by salaried managers, who report directly to him. In general, the management attitudes, practices and procedures described in relation to the Royal Oak remain valid for the group as a whole. The company's hotels are run as autonomous units, and their operations are only co-ordinated to a limited extent. Davenport maintains that the small size and geographical spread of the company's hotels makes centralized purchasing uneconomic, and that the same argument applies to the personnel function. There is no formal group reservation scheme, and although each hotel will refer custom to others within the group, this facility is little used in practice. Davenport's attitude to group marketing in general is much the same as for the Royal Oak.

Each hotel prepares its own profit and loss account. Each also submits details of closing assets and liabilities to Davenport for incorporation in the company's final accounts, which are given, with the Royal Oak's figures, later.

Peter Davenport is now 60 years old, and although he is still very much in charge, he has begun to show signs of wanting to take things more easily. He used to be involved in local community affairs (as a local authority councillor and later as a JP), but has now largely withdrawn from these activities. His wife has never been active in the business and his only child has entered another profession. Davenport is thinking of selling his interest in the company 'at some time in the not-too-distant future'.

Davenport is aware that the company's overall competitive position has been deteriorating, and that this applies particularly to the Royal Oak. He has invited you to review that hotel's operations with a view to restoring its position prior to any such sale.

You are able to collect the information detailed below over a number of informal visits, and are now required to present your preliminary conclusions and recommendations for Davenport's consideration.

KNUTSFORD

Knutsford is situated some 16 miles to the south of Manchester. It is an old market town with a good shopping centre.

There are frequent inter-city rail services to all main centres in the United Kingdom. London is two and a half hours away by train. The north–south M6 and east–west M63 motorways are both 5 miles away from the centre of the town. Ringway, Manchester's international airport, is 10 miles away.

The Lake District, the Yorkshire Dales, the Peak District and North Wales can all be reached in two hours by car, and there is easy access to swimming pools, golf courses, first-class cricket and football grounds, an ice-rink, theatres, cinemas and many other facilities.

Knutsford has a population of 14,852, but there are some 60,000 people living within 5 miles of the hotel, 600,000 within 10 miles and 1,700,000 within 15 miles. Population within Cheshire is expected to increase by 8.5 per cent within the next ten years, and the local planning department anticipates a 10 per cent increase in Knutsford itself.

Current average hourly earnings in Cheshire as compared with the North West and the rest of England are as follows:

	Cheshire	N. West	England
Full-time male employees	431.0p	405.7p	423.6p
Full-time female employees	304.1p	299.7p	311.9p

Socio-economic compositions are as follows:

	Knutsford	Cheshire	England
'Professional'	27.4	18.6%	16.8%
Skilled manual	52.9	54.6%	57.0%
Semi and unskilled	19.7	26.8%	26.2%

House ownership figures for the Knutsford municipal area are as follows:

Owner-occupied	65%
Council-owned	27%
Privately rented	8%
	100%

Car ownership per household figures for the Knutsford municipal area are as follows:

No car	26%
1 car	47%
2 or more cars	27%
	100%

FACILITIES

The Royal Oak has been Knutsford's main hotel ever since it was built in the 1890s.

The Royal Oak has 54 rooms, of which 4 are twins, 8 are doubles and 42 are singles. The public rooms include a restaurant capable of seating 100 diners, a residents' lounge and a bar. The restaurant caters for non-residents.

The hotel holds a restaurant and residential licence. As the restaurant's evening opening hours are 19.00 to 21.30 hours, no application has been made for a supper hour certificate or other extension.

The ground floor public rooms have parquet flooring with turkey-red Axminster carpet tile squares or strips. The lobby has wood-panelled walls, heavy leather-covered armchairs and brass-topped coffee tables. The residents' lounge has chintz-covered armchairs and toning linen curtains, embossed wallpaper overpainted with cream distemper, traditional glass-topped coffee tables, a Victorian writing desk in one corner and a large colour TV set in the opposite corner. The bar is furnished with leather-covered chairs and stools, glass-topped tables and, like the lounge, is decorated with sporting prints. The restaurant has the same carpeting, half-panelled walls and cream distempered wallpaper, with dark-wood tables and heavy chairs; furnishings and decor are in keeping with the general style.

The stairs and upper floor corridors have wood strip flooring with the same turkey-red Axminster strip carpeting and cream painted embossed wallpaper. The bedrooms are decorated in a variety of colour schemes. The floors have carpeted squares with linoleum surrounds and the bedroom furniture is heavy and traditional, generally of dark wood. Each bedroom has a washbasin with hot and cold water, overhead strip light and razor socket, together with a bedside lamp and telephone.

Furniture, textiles and floor coverings date from the late 1960s or earlier. The overall impression is one of rather old-fashioned comfort marred by a degree of shabbiness. This is partly because the textiles and coverings have been treated with a sodium borate solution (to increase their resistance to fire) which has had an adverse effect on their appearance, and partly because most of the paintwork needs renewing.

The management have registered the building with the local Fire Officer and the plans subsequently requested have been submitted, but to date no inspection visit has been made. Current fire precautions comprise a notice and torch in each room, a manual fire extinguisher on each floor (located on the corridor close to the stairs), and a manual fire detection system.

The building was rewired in 1973. Natural gas is used for cooking. The cold water supply is fed directly from the mains and the hot water from an indirect cylinder located in the boiler house. The heating system is old, somewhat noisy, largely uncontrolled and difficult to re-light. The boiler, situated in the cellar, is hand-fired

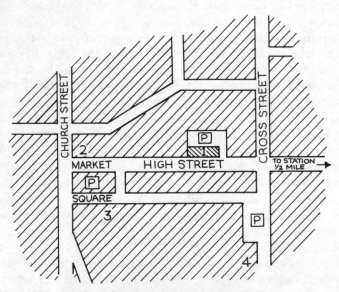

The Royal Oak, Knutsford – location plan:
1. Royal Oak Hotel
2. The Black Bull
3. Gondola Italian Restaurant
4. Restaurant Provençale (French)

using solid fuel. The distribution system is a low pressure hot water one operating by gravity.

Rooms are single-glazed throughout, and those overlooking the High Street are noisy.

The hotel is located on the High Street, some 100 yards from the central Market Square. It has parking facilities for up to 20 cars at the rear, and there is a commercial car park some 70 yards away on Church Street. Overnight street parking is usually available in Market Square or the surrounding streets, though this is either restricted or prohibited between 08.30 and 18.30 hours.

MARKET ANALYSIS

Accommodation

Registration records revealed that some 70 per cent of the guests came from south-east England. You have been given to understand that the typical guest is male, in his late fifties and involved with the chemical industry in a managerial or professional capacity. This is in accord with the home addresses given, the types of car driven (over 90 per cent of all guests arrived by car) and your own observations of guests currently in residence. A high proportion were repeat visitors who appeared to be on good terms with the reception and service staff. Bookings were typically made through the visitors' secretaries: agency bookings were infrequent and no use was made of reservation systems, either local or national.

Average daily room occupancies were as in Table 4.1.

Restaurant

The restaurant attracts businessmen and shoppers at lunchtime, including many women. An informal survey of the lunchtime customers suggests that the hotel is well established as a meeting place and that the lunches are seen as providing good value. The fact that there was no public bar and that drinks were not 'pushed' particularly attracted the female customers.

The restaurant's evening trade is admitted to be unsatisfactory. The decline (from an average of 80 covers per night in 1960 and 50 per night in 1970) had been steady and continuous. An informal survey of guests in residence reveals that the standards of the cooking and service are admitted to be high, but that the menu is thought to be unimaginative, the wine list extensive but inappropriate, and the hours inflexible. A problem pointed out by several

Table 4.1 Average daily room occupancies

	Doubles							Singles						
	Mon.	Tue.	Wed.	Thu.	Fri.	Sat.	Sun.	Mon.	Tue.	Wed.	Thu.	Fri.	Sat.	Sun.
1981														
Jan.	2.83	2.83	3.46	3.14	0.34	1.36	1.02	37.12	41.28	33.28	34.88	5.57	8.84	9.50
Feb.	3.46	3.77	2.83	3.46	1.70	0.34	1.02	39.68	34.88	38.40	33.28	4.26	7.86	10.81
Mar.	3.52	3.27	4.53	1.51	1.63	1.09	1.63	35.33	35.07	36.61	36.35	9.43	9.43	8.12
Apr.	6.60	6.60	7.24	5.34	2.38	4.42	5.10	32.96	38.08	40.96	39.36	6.88	8.84	8.52
May	7.86	5.03	6.93	7.24	2.72	4.76	3.40	33.92	34.56	36.16	33.92	9.82	6.55	6.88
Jun.	7.80	6.29	5.28	8.81	2.72	4.35	5.17	36.86	37.38	34.82	34.82	8.65	7.07	7.34
Jly	6.60	9.43	6.29	7.24	5.44	6.80	6.12	36.80	36.48	39.36	36.16	7.86	8.84	8.19
Aug.	5.98	5.03	8.50	9.43	8.16	8.50	8.16	31.36	35.20	34.56	37.44	6.55	9.50	7.86
Sep.	8.05	10.06	11.32	10.82	6.80	7.89	7.34	35.33	35.33	34.82	34.82	9.17	8.91	9.96
Oct.	7.24	6.29	5.34	4.72	3.06	5.44	5.44	31.68	34.88	34.56	35.84	8.19	7.86	6.55
Nov.	5.67	4.40	5.03	5.34	2.72	4.42	3.40	30.72	36.16	35.20	37.12	7.53	8.52	6.88
Dec.	6.04	6.29	6.79	6.04	3.54	2.72	4.08	34.05	35.84	37.12	35.33	7.86	8.38	6.81
1983														
Jan.	2.58	2.58	3.16	2.86	0.29	1.16	0.87	33.06	36.77	29.64	31.06	4.97	7.90	8.48
Feb.	3.16	3.44	2.58	3.16	1.45	0.29	0.87	35.34	31.06	34.20	29.64	3.80	7.02	9.65
Mar.	3.21	2.98	4.13	1.38	1.39	0.93	1.39	31.46	31.24	32.60	32.38	8.42	8.42	7.25
Apr.	6.02	6.02	6.60	4.87	2.03	3.77	4.35	29.35	33.92	36.48	35.06	6.14	7.90	7.61
May	7.17	4.59	6.32	6.60	2.32	4.06	2.90	30.21	30.78	32.20	30.21	8.77	5.85	6.14

Jun.	7.11	5.74	4.82	8.03	2.32	3.71	4.41	32.83	33.29	31.01	31.01	7.72	6.32	6.55
Jly	6.02	8.60	5.74	6.60	4.64	5.80	5.22	32.78	32.49	35.06	32.20	7.02	7.90	7.31
Aug.	5.45	4.59	7.75	8.60	6.96	7.25	6.96	27.93	31.35	30.78	33.34	5.85	8.48	7.02
Sep.	7.34	9.18	10.33	9.87	5.80	6.73	6.26	31.46	31.46	31.01	31.01	8.19	7.96	8.89
Oct.	6.60	5.74	4.87	4.31	2.61	4.64	4.64	28.22	31.06	30.78	31.92	7.31	7.02	5.85
Nov.	5.17	4.01	4.59	4.87	2.32	3.77	2.90	27.36	32.20	31.35	33.06	6.73	7.61	6.14
Dec.	5.51	5.74	6.20	5.51	3.02	2.32	3.48	30.32	31.92	33.06	31.46	7.02	7.49	6.08
1985														
Jan.	1.91	1.91	2.34	2.12	0.25	1.00	0.75	29.00	32.25	26.00	27.25	4.25	6.75	7.25
Feb.	2.34	2.55	1.91	2.34	1.25	0.25	0.75	31.00	27.25	30.00	26.00	3.25	6.00	8.25
Mar.	2.38	2.21	3.06	1.02	1.20	0.80	1.20	27.60	27.40	28.60	28.40	7.20	7.20	6.20
Apr.	4.46	4.46	4.89	3.61	1.75	3.25	3.75	25.75	29.75	32.00	30.75	5.25	6.75	6.50
May	5.31	3.40	4.68	4.89	2.00	3.50	2.50	26.50	27.00	28.25	26.50	7.50	5.00	5.25
Jun.	5.27	4.25	3.57	5.95	2.00	3.20	3.80	28.80	29.20	27.20	27.20	6.60	5.40	5.60
Jly	4.46	6.37	4.25	4.89	4.00	5.00	4.50	28.75	28.50	30.75	28.25	6.00	6.75	6.25
Aug.	4.04	3.40	5.74	6.37	6.00	6.25	6.00	24.50	27.50	27.00	29.25	5.00	7.25	6.00
Sep.	5.44	6.80	7.65	7.31	5.00	5.80	5.40	27.60	27.60	27.20	27.20	7.00	6.80	7.60
Oct.	4.89	4.25	3.61	3.19	2.25	4.00	4.00	24.75	27.25	27.00	28.00	6.25	6.00	5.00
Nov.	3.83	2.97	3.40	3.61	2.00	3.25	2.50	24.00	28.25	27.50	29.00	5.75	6.50	5.25
Dec.	4.08	4.25	4.59	4.08	2.60	2.00	3.00	26.60	28.00	29.00	27.60	6.00	6.40	5.20

guests is that the bar facilities are not conducive to confidential discussions with colleagues.

Competition

The main competition for the Royal Oak comes from the Black Bull, an old coaching inn also located in the town centre, and from the Leofric, a two-year-old motel located on the outskirts of the town close to both motorways. A comparison of the facilities and resources of these three establishments is given in Table 4.2.

In addition, there are at least half a dozen quality restaurants situated in Knutsford, of which two (the Gondola and the Provençale) are within easy walking distance of the Royal Oak. These provide approximately another 150–180 covers open six evenings a week. Knutsford also has over 20 public houses, most of which offer bar food/pub grub at lunchtime, at a level equivalent to the Black Bull.

The potential for evening trade is considerable, given the population figures, and you understand that this is an area into which the Leofric is expanding energetically. The Leofric is also marketing its conference facilities aggressively.

The Royal Oak, Knutsford – front view.

Table 4.2 Comparison of facilities and resources: Royal Oak and competitors

	Royal Oak	Leofric	Black Bull
Owner	Independent	National hotel chain	National brewery
Site	Town centre	Outskirts in own grounds	Town centre
Rooms	12T/D, 42S	30T, 20S	8T/D, 8S
BB rates (in £)	D:25, S:16	T:40, S:30	D:18, S:12
Service quality	Very good	Impersonal	Fair
Property condition	Reasonable	New	Fair
Conference facilities	None	Good	None
Function facilities	See restaurant data	Good for up to 100	Limited to 25 persons
Bar facilities	Diners and residents only	Diners and residents only	Full on-licence, 2 public bars
Restaurant size	100 covers	100 covers	25 covers
Evening meal	Silver service	Modern service	Traditional
Sessions per week	7	7	6
ASP: Food	£8.25	£6.00	£4.50
ASP: Drink	£3.50	£2.00	£1.50
Covers per day	25	50	8
Functions per month	2	6	1
Lunch	Informal	Bistro type	Bar snacks
Sessions per week	6	6	6
ASP: Food	£3.00	£3.00	£2.25
ASP: Drink	£0.70	£0.70	£0.70
Covers per day	150	75	45
Wine list	Extensive	Limited	Limited
ASP (Wines only)	£6.80	£5.50	£4.10
AA/RAC Class	2 star	2 star	1 star

Acorn Hotels Ltd: Balance Sheet as at 31/10/1985

	Royal Oak 1985		Royal Oak 1984		Acorn Hotels Ltd 1985		Acorn Hotels Ltd 1984	
	£	£	£	£	£	£	£	£
Fixed assets:								
Land and buildings		240,000		240,000		725,000		725,000
Fixtures and fittings	89,000		89,000		285,000		250,000	
Less Depreciation	76,500	12,500	68,900	20,100	219,750	65,250	198,750	51,250
Motor vehicles	15,000		15,000		42,650		42,650	
Less Depreciation	6,000	9,000	3,500	11,500	16,670	25,980	9,850	32,800
Net fixed assets		261,500		271,600		816,230		809,050
Current assets:								
Wet stocks	7,500		7,200		21,600		20,800	
Dry stocks	4,500		4,500		13,650		13,700	
Debtors	3,825		3,136		11,620		10,205	
Bank	450	16,275	3,750	18,586	5,535	52,405	17,512	62,217

Less Current liabilities:								
Bank overdraft	2,370							
Creditors	16,605	18,975	—	14,132	—	42,637	—	40,656
Net current assets		(2,700)		4,454		9,768		21,561
Total assets		258,800		276,054		825,998		830,611
Less Long-term liabilities:						85,000		75,000
Total						£740,998		£755,611
Share capital and reserves:								
Share capital, authorized and issued:								
100,000 Ordinary shares of £1 each						200,000		200,000
Share premium account						50,000		50,000
Revaluation reserve						315,000		315,000
Profit and loss account						175,998		190,611
Total						£740,998		£755,611

Notes:

1. Land and buildings are shown at surveyor's valuation dated 1983.

2. Fixtures and fittings and motor vehicles are shown at cost less aggregate depreciation to date.

Acorn Hotels Ltd: Profit and Loss Account for Year Ended 31/10/1985

| | Royal Oak | | | | Acorn Hotels Ltd | | | |
| | 1985 | | 1984 | | 1985 | | 1984 | |
	£	£	£	£	£	£	£	£
Turnover		429,138		409,827		1,445,512		1,390,064
Cost of sales:								
Purchases	125,308		124,750		371,973		367,964	
Wages	156,635	281,943	129,557	254,307	438,905	810,878	389,462	757,426
Gross profit		147,195		155,520		634,634		632,638
Establishment expenses:								
Rates	10,200		8,100		29,780		22,350	
Light & heat	14,970		13,350		42,556		39,785	
Cleaning etc.	12,273		11,587		36,932		34,525	
Repairs etc.	32,700		29,997		94,200		83,420	
Sundries	8,282	78,425	7,896	70,930	26,764	230,232	25,874	205,954
Administrative expenses:								
Telephone	2,060		1,674		6,345		5,222	
Advertising etc.	4,248		4,206		15,664		13,550	
Insurance	8,950		8,450		25,778		24,553	
Motor expenses	2,446		1,888		7,250		5,560	

Subscriptions	429		386		1,550		1,248	
Audit fees	3,646		3,288		10,938		9,500	
Managers' salaries	20,000	41,779	18,000	37,892	72,000	139,525	66,000	125,633
Financial expenses:								
Bank charges	1,245		944		3,600		2,800	
Bank interest	5,193		4,506		7,500		10,525	
Loan interest					10,125		10,687	
Bad debts	1,631		944		3,504		1,884	
Depreciation: motor	2,500		2,500		6,800		7,500	
Depreciation: fixtures and fittings	7,600	18,169	7,600	16,494	14,000	45,529	14,000	47,396
Directors' salaries					25,000		22,250	
Total expenditure		420,316		379,623		1,251,164		1,158,659
Net profit/loss		8,822		30,204		194,348		231,405
Taxation					77,739		92,562	
P&L b/fwd					40,611		48,232	
Dividend					50,000		50,000	
P&L c/fwd					25,998		40,611	
Total						£194,348		£231,405

Notes to Profit and Loss Account

1. The Royal Oak's managers' salaries were paid to Peter Davenport and his wife.

2. Directors' salaries were paid to Peter Davenport and his wife.

3. The Royal Oak's advertising expenditure for 1985 was analysed as follows:

Item	Location	No.	Time	Cost (£)
New sign	Hotel front	1	All year	2,200.00
Newsletter	Past guests	400	Sep./Feb.	165.00
Guest matches	Rooms	1,500	All year	80.00
Magazine ad.	County	12	Monthly	975.00
Menu folder	In hotel	100	All year	525.00
Tent cards	In hotel	100	All year	50.00
Brochure	Enquirers	800	All year	225.00
Shopping guide	Local	12	Monthly	28.00
				£4,248.00

STAFFING

Employee Analysis

Job	Sex	Nationality	Age	Employment (years)	Rate (£/week)
Manager	M	UK	61	30	200
Assistant manager (manager's wife)	F	UK	59	30	180
Secretary	F	UK	26	1	100
Receptionist	F	UK	42	8	110
Assistant receptionist	F	UK	30	2	95
P/t assistant receptionist (1)	F	UK	38	5	55

P/t assistant receptionist (2)	F	UK	50	0.5	50
Housekeeper	F	UK	57	12	120
Assistant housekeeper (1)	F	UK	45	10	60
Assistant housekeeper (2)	F	Eire	48	5	60
Assistant housekeeper (3)	F	UK	36	0.5	60
P/t cleaner	F	Eire	52	2	40
Porter	M	UK	60	27	100
Assistant porter	M	UK	52	5	80
Maintenance man	M	UK	47	2.5	100
Barman	M	Eire	50	3	110
P/t barman (1)	M	UK	43	1.5	60
P/t barman (2)	M	UK	59	0.5	60
Head/wine waiter	M	UK	58	18	155
Waiter (1)	M	UK	53	4	95
Waiter (2)	M	UK	49	2	95
Waiter (3)	M	Spain	25	0.5	95
Commis waiter (1)	M	Spain	28	1.5	60
Commis waiter (2)	M	Italy	24	1	60
Commis waiter (3)	M	UK	24	0.5	60
Commis waiter (4)	F	UK	36	5	60
Commis waiter (5)	F	UK	30	4	60
Commis waiter (6)	F	UK	22	1	60
Still room hand	F	UK	56	8	80
Chef	M	UK	56	18	185
2nd chef	M	UK	49	10	145
Commis chef	M	UK	24	0.5	82
Apprentice chef	M	UK	17	0.5	40
Kitchen porter (1)	M	Poland	58	6	70
Kitchen porter (2)	M	Eire	32	0.5	70

The hotel does not operate a service charge, but you are given to understand that guests in fact tip generously. These tips benefit the restaurant, bar and portering staff, with the housekeeping staff also receiving a certain amount. The restaurant staff operate a tronc system (this does not include the still room hand) but you have no details as to the amounts involved.

Staff Notes

Peter Davenport (the owner/manager) is respected by the staff, who consider him to be fair, and is on good terms with his guests, many of whom share his public school and service background. His philosophy of management may be summed up as 'Pick a good team and let them get on with it', and his attitude to marketing as 'Good wine needs no bush'. He makes himself available to meet guests and also provides cover when necessary, particularly in reception and in the restaurant.

Tom Harvey, the Chef, is well qualified and has worked in top-class hotels in both Britain and Europe. He is honest and a good craftsman, committed to high standards of preparation and presentation, but otherwise generally easygoing. According to the apprentice chef, the Royal Oak is a good place to learn one's trade – 'Chef knows what he's doing and is prepared to help you, but he doesn't push you *too* hard' – though the commis chef criticizes Tom for not being adventurous enough – 'He reckons all he has to do is to keep on producing good plain food and the customers'll keep coming, but the fact is that it's dull.' However, Tom gets on well with the second chef, who shares his general outlook, and this sets the tone of the kitchen.

Vernon Russell, the head/wine waiter, is a Londoner who married a local woman and has settled down in Knutsford. He has built up an extensive wine list in close co-operation with Peter Davenport, and is knowledgeable and enthusiastic about it. He is competent, but, like Tom, inclined to be easygoing. You form the impression that the two of them do not actively encourage function bookings which are likely to go on until after 23.00 hours. Vernon's team appear contented enough. He himself admits that both the continental staff and the locally recruited waitresses are skilful, but privately he regrets that it is no longer possible to find enough male British waiters, as he feels this would 'look better'. He is resigned to a fairly high turnover of the younger foreign waiters, who he claims only come to learn English and are frequently tempted away to city-centre establishments.

Agnes Miller, the Housekeeper, is a perfectionist, and the linen, furnishings and carpets are always immaculately clean. She is separated, with a grown-up son. She is a strong-minded woman who brooks no interference in her department: on the other hand, she does not involve herself in other people's. The two longer serving assistant housekeepers are familiar with her ways, but she has found it difficult to keep a third for any length of time, and the present incumbent appears sullen and resentful.

Sheila Martin, the Receptionist, is, by way of contrast, a notably warm, friendly personality. She trained as a typist and learned reception duties on the job at the Royal Oak. She is on excellent terms with all the regular guests, and looks after them in a way which is almost maternal. On the other hand, she finds it difficult to take much interest in financial control, which means that there are sometimes errors in bills, and her unwillingness to ask walk-in guests for a deposit has led to the occasional bad debt.

Harry Gresty, the Porter, is ex-Navy. He is cheerful, hard working and gregarious, with a good sense of humour, and is also very popular with the regular guests, who regard him as something of an institution. He is a widower, with no family and few interests outside the hotel: as a result, he is prepared to work for long hours and generally acts as night porter during the week. The assistant porter is a much less colourful personality whose main tasks are to clean the public rooms and to cover the boiler along with the maintenance/odd-job man.

Tim Corrigan, the Barman, is another somewhat colourless personality who appears to have no strong views on anything other than racing form, of which he is a devoted follower. However, he is competent and honest enough.

Sally Hawes, the Secretary, is a young woman, recently married, who trained as a stenographer and who worked previously for a building firm. She deals with all routine business other than reservations, keeps the general accounts and calculates wages. She gets on well enough with Sheila Martin, though the two have occasional differences of opinion because of Sheila's somewhat more slapdash approach to accounting matters.

ADMINISTRATION

The Royal Oak is owned by Acorn Hotels, a limited company, but the major shareholders are Peter Davenport and his wife and in practice the hotel is managed solely by Davenport.

Davenport co-ordinates the hotel's activities through regular weekly meetings of the senior staff (Tom Harvey, Vernon Russell, Agnes Miller and Sheila Martin). These meetings are informal: in other words, the four staff members expect to assemble in Davenport's office on Monday morning, but there is no agenda and the proceedings are not minuted.

Discussions deal with the co-ordination of activities and the settlement of operational problems on an *ad hoc* basis. Typical topics include arrangements for special events such as the occasional group tour booking or function, the repair or renewal of equipment, the replacement of staff who have retired or resigned and the renegotiation of purchasing contracts. The senior staff trust each other to keep the substance of these conversations confidential, and they are invariably frank. Staff performance is discussed at some length, though since there is no formal training scheme or disciplinary procedure the usual result of any dissatisfaction is that Davenport says he will 'speak to' the offender.

Davenport and his departmental heads usually have certain standard reports available at these meetings. Sheila Martin prepares daily occupancy summaries showing room/bed percentages and tabular ledger summaries. Agnes Miller maintains very full and accurate records of materials received and issued, together with comprehensive housekeeping staffing schedules. Tom Harvey prepares a cost and sales report weekly. This simply shows total sales (based on the waiters' checks, which have been checked against cash receipts and any credit bills) and cost of food sold (based on an analysed kitchen day book which records opening stocks, purchases and closing stocks). Staff meals are regarded as a part of the food cost and not recorded separately. Vernon Russell is responsible for liquor control. He maintains a master wine list and a beverage control book (this records opening stocks, purchases/returns and issues to bar/restaurant, the latter cross-checked against Corrigan's daily bar consumption summary sheets and/or waiters' checks).

The hotel does not operate a budgetary control system. Monthly departmental trading accounts are prepared by Peter Davenport and Sally Hawes, but these are not issued as a matter of routine, though Davenport discusses any unfavourable trends with the departmental head should the need arise. The final accounts are prepared by a firm of local accountants, who also do the annual stock-taking.

PLANS

Plans of the Royal Oak are provided (see pages 47 and 48).

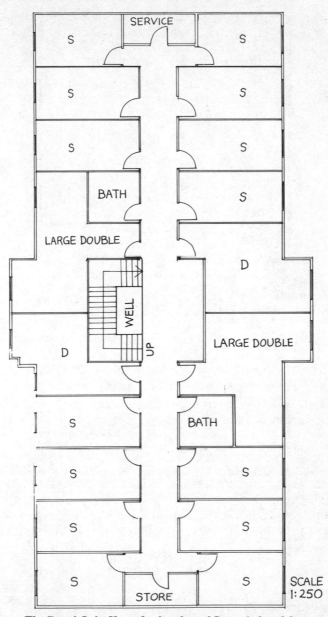

The Royal Oak, Knutsford – plan of floors 1, 2 and 3.

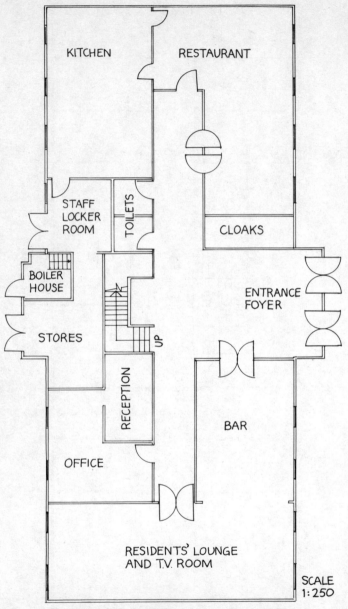

The Royal Oak, Knutsford – plan of ground floor.

INSTRUCTIONS

Peter Davenport has requested your advice. You are required to write a report:

1. analysing the current situation with regard to Acorn Hotels in general and the Royal Oak in particular;

2. submitting your recommendations for the future.

SUGGESTIONS

Your report might usefully include:

- A financial analysis and forecast

- A statistical analysis of the Royal Oak's occupancies

- A marketing analysis and outline marketing scheme

- An analysis of the existing manpower resources, with proposals regarding retraining and/or redeployment if appropriate

- A critical appraisal of the existing facilities, together with re-design proposals and plans relating to the same

- Outline building and equipment cost and installation schedules

- Capital financing and budget proposals

- Conclusions and recommendations with regard to Davenport's management procedures and practices.

CHAPTER 5

THE CHESHIRE RESTAURANTS CASE

The Royal Oak introduced you to some of the complexities of co-ordinating financial and statistical data with details of the premises and the personal particulars of the key staff. However, it was limited to one particular unit. Our next case introduces you to the complexities of multi-unit operation. It also raises some of the problems involved in deciding how best to implement an organization's strategy.

Some cases might be summed up as 'What have they been doing wrong and how can they be put right?' Others take a reasonably successful company and ask, in effect 'Which way should they go now?' This is very much the situation here. Evaluating the options will involve you in trying to make sense of builder's estimates and technical specifications, but this is very much what managers have to do in real life, and we make no apology for getting you to do it too.

Again, you will see that we have located our imaginary units in real towns. The demographic data we have provided is accurate enough, but no resemblance to any existing restaurant chain is intended.

CASE STUDY

INTRODUCTION

Cheshire Restaurants was formed by David Hughes in 1978 to run his family's expanding restaurant business. At that time it had two units located in Wilmslow and Knutsford. During the following two years further restaurants were acquired in Lymm and Northwich.

Since 1982 the Board of Directors has consisted of David Hughes and his two children. Each runs one of the restaurants, and also takes responsibility for a major functional area. The division of responsibilities is as follows:

Board member	Age	Restaurant	Functional responsibility
David Hughes	60	Wilmslow	Marketing and staff development
John Hughes	36	Knutsford	Production
Anne Hughes	32	Lymm	Finance

The Northwich restaurant is run by a salaried manager. All four restaurants are situated near the main shopping and business centres in each town and have the advantage of accessible car parking. All have restaurant licences. They are operated independently, but some attempt has been made to standardize menus, develop common staff training schemes, install similar equipment and make bulk purchasing arrangements. The accounting systems have been standardized to allow comparisons to be made.

The group's main product is a range of casserole-based meals, which are currently prepared within each restaurant to standard recipes. There are no competitors providing precisely this range of dishes in any of the four locations.

When the company was formed, the Board of Directors agreed that one of its objectives should be to expand as and when opportunity offered. It set as a target the ownership and operation of six such restaurants in the Cheshire area by the end of 1988.

The company's shares are held entirely within the family. David Hughes and his wife currently hold 60 per cent, the two children 20 per cent each.

At a board meeting in December 1985 two separate proposals were tabled. They were:

1. The development of a central cook-chill facility to be located at a unit yet to be decided, to service both that and the group's other restaurants.

2. The purchase of basement premises in Altrincham (previously used for the storage of bank records) with a view to converting them into a restaurant to be called 'The Altrincham Cellar'.

The Board agreed that the maximum amount it could afford to invest in 1986 was £80,000. The meeting was then adjourned to allow time for further consideration.

Financial information relating to Cheshire Restaurants Ltd for the past three years is provided below, together with preliminary papers relating to the two proposals.

CHESHIRE RESTAURANTS LTD: FINANCIAL INFORMATION

Profit and Loss Accounts for Years Ended 31 December 1983, 1984 and 1985

	1983 £	1984 £	1985 £
Food sales	465,822	499,322	527,748
Less Cost of sales	177,519	194,007	208,669
Gross food profit	288,303	305,315	319,079
Beverage sales	103,507	114,543	124,253
Less Cost of sales	49,412	54,640	59,663
Gross beverage profit	54,095	59,903	64,590
Gross profit	342,398	365,218	383,669
Less Wages and salaries	149,200	165,100	173,800
Net margin	193,198	200,118	209,869
Heat, light, power	15,192	15,558	16,793
Advertising	6,915	7,341	8,104
Administrative expenses	11,727	12,728	13,372
General expenses	12,000	12,664	13,280
Rent, rates, insurance	9,944	10,779	11,729
Depreciation	4,350	4,700	4,700
Financial expenses	8,696	6,135	3,522
Total overhead expenses	68,824	69,905	71,500
Profit before taxation	124,374	130,213	138,369
Taxation	52,237	50,132	50,343
Dividends paid and proposed	62,500	62,500	62,500
Retained profit	£9,637	£17,581	£25,526

Balance Sheets as at 31 December 1983, 1984, 1985

	1983 £	1984 £	1985 £
Fixed assets	718,000	713,300	708,600
Current assets:			
Stock	13,469	16,582	18,936
Cash	15,203	14,298	13,519
	28,672	30,880	32,455
Current liabilities	11,202	13,600	17,005
Net current assets	17,470	17,280	15,450
Net assets	735,470	730,580	724,050
Loans	56,000	38,500	20,000
Totals	£679,470	£692,080	£704,050
Share capital	500,000	500,000	500,000
Profit and loss a/c	179,470	192,080	204,050
Totals	£679,470	£692,080	£704,050

Branch Profit and Loss Accounts for Years Ended 31 December 1983, 1984 and 1985

	Knutsford			Northwich		
	1983 £	1984 £	1985 £	1983 £	1984 £	1985 £
Food sales	113,689	126,287	134,957	110,367	124,658	133,459
Less Cost of sales	43,187	50,276	55,856	39,173	45,587	49,167
Gross profit on food	70,502	76,011	79,101	71,194	79,071	84,292
Beverage sales	24,569	26,165	27,902	10,314	15,167	17,289
Less Cost of sales	12,177	12,994	13,896	4,602	7,057	8,180
Gross profit on beverage	12,392	13,171	14,006	5,712	8,110	9,109
Gross profit	82,894	89,182	93,107	76,906	87,181	93,401
Less Wages and salaries	36,700	39,200	40,800	30,500	36,500	39,200
Net margin	46,194	49,982	52,307	46,406	50,681	54,201
Heat, light, power	2,948	3,078	3,268	3,803	4,034	4,126
Advertising	2,106	2,196	2,488	1,137	1,193	1,236
Administrative expenses	2,695	3,075	3,246	3,080	3,186	3,274
General expenses	2,189	2,353	2,553	2,812	2,923	3,192
Rent, rates, insurance	2,156	2,346	2,555	2,806	3,214	3,424
Depreciation	1,000	1,000	1,000	1,000	1,000	1,000
Financial expenses	2,793	1,865	1,057	1,807	1,518	1,235
Total overhead expenses	15,887	15,913	16,167	16,445	17,068	17,487
Net profit	£30,307	£34,069	£36,140	£29,961	£33,613	£36,714

	Lymm			Wilmslow		
	1983 £	1984 £	1985 £	1983 £	1984 £	1985 £
Food sales	101,792	103,579	110,768	139,974	144,798	148,564
Less Cost of sales	44,003	45,487	48,449	51,156	52,657	55,197
Gross profit on food	57,789	58,092	62,319	88,818	92,141	93,367
Beverage sales	27,568	29,535	31,841	41,056	43,676	47,221
Less Cost of sales	13,560	14,042	15,553	19,073	20,547	22,034
Gross profit on beverage	14,008	15,493	16,288	21,983	23,129	25,187
Gross profit	71,797	73,585	78,607	110,801	115,270	118,554
Less Wages and salaries	31,500	33,700	36,500	50,500	55,700	57,300
Net margin	40,297	39,885	42,107	60,301	59,570	61,254
Heat, light, power	3,306	3,198	3,612	5,135	5,248	5,787
Advertising	895	1,068	1,387	2,777	2,884	2,993
Administrative expenses	2,750	2,936	3,112	3,202	3,531	3,740
General expenses	3,003	3,156	3,287	3,996	4,232	4,248
Rent, rates, insurance	2,214	2,134	2,450	2,768	3,085	3,300
Depreciation	850	1,000	1,000	1,500	1,700	1,700
Financial expenses	2,471	1,624	617	1,625	1,128	613
Total overhead expenses	15,489	15,116	15,465	21,003	21,808	22,381
Net profit	£24,808	£24,769	£26,642	£39,298	£37,762	£38,873

Branch Assets and Liabilities as at 31 December 1983, 1984, 1985

	Knutsford			Northwich		
	1983 £	1984 £	1985 £	1983 £	1984 £	1985 £
Fixed assets	183,000	182,000	181,000	145,000	144,000	143,000
Current assets:						
Stock	2,794	3,044	3,126	2,456	2,735	2,887
Cash	3,013	2,563	2,604	3,188	3,609	3,757
	5,807	5,607	5,730	5,644	6,344	6,644
Current liabilities	2,600	3,474	4,096	3,622	3,651	3,913
Net current assets	3,207	2,133	1,634	2,022	2,693	2,731
Net assets	186,207	184,133	182,634	147,022	146,693	145,731
Loans	18,000	12,000	6,000	12,000	10,000	8,000
	£168,207	£172,133	£176,634	£135,022	£136,693	£137,731

	Lymm			Wilmslow		
	1983 £	1984 £	1985 £	1983 £	1984 £	1985 £
Fixed assets	170,000	169,000	168,000	220,000	218,300	216,600
Current assets:						
Stock	3,545	5,747	7,706	4,674	5,056	5,217
Cash	4,963	4,128	3,319	4,039	3,998	3,839
	8,508	9,875	11,025	8,713	9,054	9,056
Current liabilities	2,413	3,699	5,533	2,567	2,776	3,463
Net current assets	6,095	6,176	5,492	6,146	6,278	5,593
Net assets	176,095	175,176	173,492	226,146	224,578	222,193
Loans	16,000	10,000	3,000	10,000	6,500	3,000
	£160,095	£165,176	£170,492	£216,146	£218,078	£219,193

To: Members, Cheshire Restaurant Board of Directors

From: John Hughes

Date: December 1985

Proposal to Set up a Cook-chill System

Introduction

A firm such as Cheshire Restaurants operating within a limited geographical area and with a standardized menu ought to be able to derive two important advantages from adopting a centralized production process:

1. Maintenance of food quality
2. A reduction in staff costs.

I apologize for the fact that delays in obtaining some of the necessary information have made it impossible to produce detailed cost estimates, but the considerations listed below should enable us to determine whether such a change would be worthwhile.

Current Demand (per week)

	Northwich	Knutsford	Lymm	Wilmslow	Totals
Midday	320	380	260	380	1,340
Evening	190	260	240	420	1,110
Totals	510	640	500	800	2,450

The average weight per portion is 125 g.

Operating Considerations

The equipment required would include a blast chiller, central production coldstores, end kitchen chill store cabinets and miscellaneous items (e.g. trolleys and containers).

Equipment life is estimated at 5 years.

Equipment could be located at any of the existing restaurants without serious dislocation or additional expense.

Power costs may be assumed to be 5.5p per kw/hr.

We would also require a refrigerated van for distribution purposes. A 10 ton van will cost £20,000. It can carry 14 insulated boxes, each holding 300 portions. Each such box would cost £400. Normal van operating costs (i.e. insurance, licence and servicing) can be assumed to be c. £1,000 per annum. In addition, it would consume liquid nitrogen for cooling purposes at approximately £20 per trip.

Staffing
Additional labour costs in respect of the central production unit are estimated at £12,000 per annum.

In addition, we would require a van driver. His wages can be estimated at £8,000 per annum. He would be expected to help in the kitchen stores when not delivering.

These expenses would be offset by a reduction in unit labour costs. The approximate savings per unit can be assumed to be 1 chef at £6,000 per annum per unit.

Frazer Freezers Co. plc: Equipment Specifications

Blast Chillers

Production capacities:

	FCB45	FCB90	FCB130	FCB180	FCB360
Capacity per chilling cycle (lb)	45	90	130	180	360
Capacity per chilling cycle (kg)	20	40	60	81	162
Chilling time (average hours)	1.5	1.5	1.5	1.5	1.5
No. of chillings per 8 hr day	4	4	4	4	4

Power and extraction rates:

	Power (kw)	*Extraction rate*
FCB45	1.6	545 kcal per hour
FCB90	4.6	2,016 kcal per hour
FCB130	6.6	3,276 kcal per hour
FCB180	13.0	6,045 kcal per hour
FCB360	27.0	12,600 kcal per hour

Central Production Coldstores

Insulation thickness	120 mm
Thermal conductivity of insulation	25 mJ/msec °C
Standard height	2.59 m

Trolley Capacities
Based on chilling trolleys 765 mm long by 670 mm wide with 12 tiers of containers:

Trolleys	*Containers (No.)*	*Width (Metres)*	*Depth (Metres)*	*Capacity (Cu. metres)*
Single aisle:				
4	96	2.92	1.75	10.80
8	192	2.92	3.21	20.66
12	288	2.92	4.67	30.52
16	384	2.92	6.13	40.38
20	480	2.92	7.60	50.24
Double aisle:				
8	192	5.55	1.75	21.05
16	384	5.55	3.21	40.26
24	576	5.55	4.67	58.92
32	768	5.55	6.13	77.29
40	960	5.55	7.60	85.90

Stainless Steel Dishes
Capacity: 25 portions

End Kitchen Chill Store Cabinets

Model	Containers (No.)	Max. food weight	Size (W×D×H)	Capacity (litres)
FSC50	28	95.5 kg	680×806×1,715 mm	500
FSC60	34	116.0 kg	680×806×2,083 mm	600
FSC120	56	191.0 kg	1,397×806×1,715 mm	1,125
FSC140	72	245.5 kg	2,115×806×2,083 mm	1,350
FSC200	108	368.0 kg	2,115×806×2,083 mm	2,100

Note: Standard insulation thickness 40 mm

Frazer Freezers Co. plc: Price List

	£
FCB45 Blast chiller	2,000
FCB90 Blast chiller	4,320
FCB130 Blast chiller	5,300
FCB180 Blast chiller	8,800
FCB360 Blast chiller	14,500
4 Trolley CPC (single aisle)	3,420
8 Trolley CPC (single aisle)	4,600
12 Trolley CPC (single aisle)	5,400
16 Trolley CPC (single aisle)	7,450
20 Trolley CPC (single aisle)	9,000
8 Trolley CPC (double aisle)	4,550
16 Trolley CPC (double aisle)	7,350
24 Trolley CPC (double aisle)	9,900
32 Trolley CPC (double aisle)	12,050
40 Trolley CPC (double aisle)	14,200
Trolleys (each)	450
Stainless steel dishes (each)	30
FSC50 End kitchen CSC	1,050
FSC60 End kitchen CSC	1,075
FSC120 End kitchen CSC	1,440
FSC140 End kitchen CSC	1,675
FSC200 End kitchen CSC	3,150

To: Members, Cheshire Restaurant Board of Directors

From: David Hughes

Date: December 1985

Proposal to Purchase the Altrincham Cellar

I wish to propose the purchase of the cellar premises at No. 15, Edgar Street, Altrincham, with a view to developing a new restaurant there.

I am advised that we can purchase the freehold of this property for £40,000.

The Site (see plans included in Appendix IV)

The Cellar is situated in the basement of a building owned by a local estate agent and on the fringe of the main shopping area. A large number of people pass by during shopping hours, and the area also attracts pedestrians in the evening. The whole area is below ground level and is entered by descending stairs. This will all add to the atmosphere and enable the creation of a distinctive meal experience.

The premises were previously used for the storage of bank records. They have been vacant for three months. Negotiations for sale to a would-be bistro owner had reached an advanced stage but fell through eventually because he was unable to raise the necessary capital, and the owners are anxious for a quick sale. Outline planning permission for restaurant use has already been approved.

The premises have been newly plastered and are in a good state of cleanliness. They have an independent gas central heating system (installed by the bank as an aid to temperature control) and access through the rear to a service and delivery area which is also used by refuse collection vehicles. All mains services are available.

Adequate street and multi-storey parking facilities are available within easy walking distance.

I have consulted Messrs Mason and Co. and obtained an outline builder's estimate for necessary work prior to furnishing (see below). Obviously, decisions about kitchen equipment and the type of decor and furnishings thought most appropriate in terms of market and image will still have to be made, and will affect the overall cost.

On the basis of our previous experience, we need to allow six weeks from date of order for the delivery, assembly and installation of kitchen equipment and furnishings.

Sundry Appendices relating to this proposal are also provided below.

Appendix I

Mason and Co. (Builders)
Wilmslow
Cheshire

Cheshire Restaurants Ltd.
Northwich
Cheshire

December 1985

ESTIMATE

To:	£
Preparation of site: Clearing and cleaning	300
Providing and installing necessary electrical fittings together with signs	600
Installation of toilets	1,200
Building in sinks, refrigeration units, etc.	2,000
Total	4,100

NB: This estimate is provisional only, and the amounts quoted should be confirmed as and when detailed plans and schedules become available.

Providing sufficient advance notice is given, the work of preparing and decorating the site should take approximately five weeks.

Appendix II – Market Survey of Altrincham

Note: For the purposes of this survey Altrincham is deemed to include both Altrincham itself and the neighbouring districts of Bowdon and Hale for whom Altrincham is the natural shopping centre.

1. Location

Altrincham is well served by the transport system. It lies close to both the main M6 (North–South), M62 (East–West Trans–Pennine) and M56 (Chester and North Wales) motorways. The town

63

itself is 8 miles from Manchester and is convenient for the industrial centres of the Mersey.

The town is located close to Manchester's international Ringway Airport.

It has excellent train and bus services to Manchester and surrounding centres. The railway and bus stations are close to the site.

2. Population

(a) Trends:

	1961	1971	1981	1991 (est.)
Altrincham	41,030	41,067	42,215	46,000
Bowdon	4,380	4,929	5,945	7,500
Hale	14,690	17,194	17,619	19,000
Total	60,100	63,190	65,779	72,500

(b) By age (1971):

	Altrincham		Hale		Bowdon	
	No.	%	No.	%	No.	%
0–4 years	3,263	7.9	1,153	6.7	327	6.6
5–17 years	7,847	19.1	3,799	22.1	1,040	21.1
18–64 years	24,298	59.2	9,911	57.6	2,807	57.0
65+ years	5,659	13.8	2,331	13.6	755	15.3
Total	41,067	100.0	17,194	100.0	4,929	100.0

(c) By sex (1971):

	Altrincham		Hale		Bowdon	
	No.	%	No.	%	No.	%
Males	19,657	47.8	8,253	46.0	2,215	44.9
Females	21,410	52.2	8,941	54.0	2,714	55.1
Total	41,067	100.0	17,194	100.0	4,929	100.0

(d) By occupation (actual figures 1971):

	Altrincham No.	Hale No.	Bowdon No.
Professional	840	310	670
Employers/managers	1,870	350	1,370
Foreman	5,260	270	970
Non-manual	2,950	270	1,350
Semi-skilled	1,670	80	370

3. Sources of Demand

These can be divided into the following groups:

(a) *Commerce.* The emphasis near the site itself is mainly on the service industries. There are many business and professional offices, such as financial, banking, insurance services, estate agents and solicitors.

(b) *Industry.* This is relatively limited, though there are a few hundred employed in manufacturing industry nearby.

(c) *Shopping.* Altrincham serves as the main shopping centre for a wide area. The shops are concentrated in the centre, which means that many local inhabitants live nearby. A large proportion of those are in the middle to upper income brackets, and their relatively high average age means that the majority do not have dependent children, thus giving them even more disposable income. It is claimed that Altrincham has the second highest capital income in the country. With a population of 40,752 (1971 census) and 541 retail outlets, the average annual spend per inhabitant in 1972 was £462 as compared with £367 in Wilmslow and a regional average of £274 (Census of Distribution 1971).

(d) *Local residential trade.* In view of the high local disposable income, the potential for an evening dining-out market is clearly high.

4. Competition

Every competitor within 20 minutes of walking time was visited, and we can report that lunchtime trade was good to excellent, and that those restaurants remaining open in the evening were well patronized. By taking a count every 30 minutes we established that catering units in the area were covering their seats 250 per cent at lunch time and 100 per cent in the evening.

Establishments were obviously catering for a different market in the evening, and it can be assumed that customers were prepared to spend more time and to pay more for a different 'meal experience'.

Our survey indicated that wine sales in the evenings were high.

Appendix III – The Altrincham Cellar: Estimated Operating Figures

Rates are £3,500 per annum.

Daily turnover rates are expected to be as follows in Year 1:

	Midday	*Evenings*
Monday	1.0	0.5
Tuesday	1.0	0.5
Wednesday	1.5	0.5
Thursday	2.5	1.0
Friday	3.0	1.0
Saturday	3.5	1.0
Average	2.0	0.75

These turnover rates can be expected to rise to 2.5 (midday) and 1.00 (evening) in Year 2.

Expected demand in terms of our current Cheshire Restaurants menu is as follows:

	Cost	*Price* *(ex VAT)*	*Demand (% covers)*	
			Midday	*Evening*
Soup of the Day	21p	50p	15	10
Corn on the Cob	23p	75p	3	6
Spare Ribs	24p	43p	2	3
Pâté	42p	90p	3	10
Prawn Cocktail	52p	£1.20	3	17
Stuffed Mushrooms	35p	85p	3	8
Melon Tropicana	97p	£1.95	4	14
Avocado with Prawns	80p	£1.60	4	12
Beef Stroganoff	£1.43	£3.25	7	15
Lancashire Hot Pot	92p	£1.95	17	3
Hawaiian Ham Casserole	£1.32	£2.95	5	14
Chicken & Pork Hot Pot	£1.17	£2.75	6	13

	Cost	Price (ex VAT)	Demand (% covers) Midday	Evening
Gamekeeper's Casserole	£1.32	£3.00	5	13
Veal Fricasse	£1.30	£2.85	8	11
Duck Casserole	£1.18	£2.95	5	13
Chicken Casserole	84p	£1.90	16	6
Chicken Curry	78p	£1.80	15	4
Chicken & Fish Casserole	82p	£1.95	16	8
Sweet Trolley	45p	£1.10	18	65
Pastries	33p	80p	10	24
Coffee	17p	70p	55	75

Overall food costs are expected to be 40% of selling costs.

Expected drinks sales (% of covers):

	Midday	Evening
Beers	20%	10%
Wines (bottles)	15%	30%
Wines (by glass)	15%	40%

Currently house wine costs £1.88 and sells at £3.50. The same wine sold per glass (6 per bottle) is priced at 60p per glass. Better quality wines cost on average £2.20 per bottle and sell at £4.70.

Staff costs have not been estimated. These will depend on:

1. The number of covers which the Cellar can accommodate

2. Whether self-service or waiter/waitress service is required.

Observations made of competitors suggest that lunchtime self-service and evening waiter/waitress service would be acceptable.

Appendix IV
Plans for the Altrincham Cellar are provided (see pages 68–69).

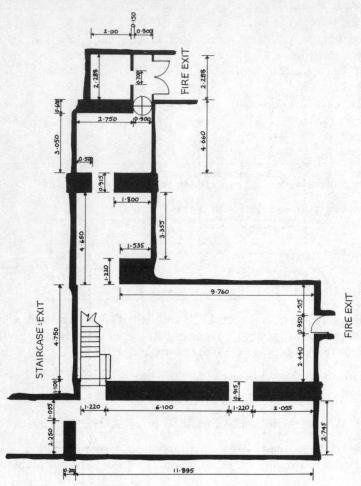

The Altrincham Cellar – site plan.

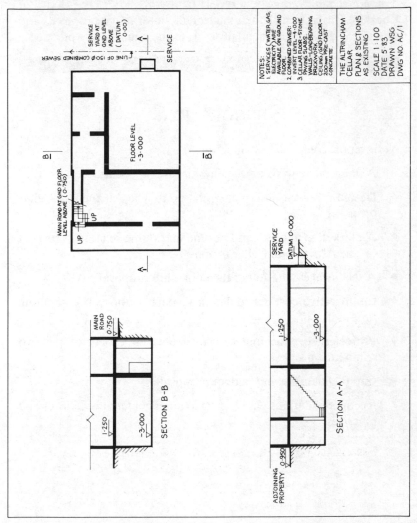

The Altrincham Cellar – plan of cellar existing.

INSTRUCTIONS

You are required to write a report for submission to the Board of Cheshire Restaurants Ltd, analysing the alternative proposals and submitting your recommendations as to the course to be pursued.

SUGGESTIONS

Your report could usefully include:

- A financial analysis of the Cheshire Restaurants accounts

- Design proposals and plans relating to The Altrincham Cellar proposal

- A marketing analysis and outline marketing scheme in respect of The Altrincham Cellar proposal

- A technical evaluation of the cook-chill proposal

- Comparative cost schedules in respect of the two competing proposals

- Projected revenue and cost estimates in respect of the two competing proposals

- Capital financing and budget proposals

- Recommendations with regard to management procedures and practices.

CHAPTER 6

THE DEE HALL CASE

Our next case might appear to be a return to the single unit problem, but it is actually more complex than that. The Dee Hall is larger than the Royal Oak, and the management has to grapple with the organizational problems involved in a change of ownership while simultaneously deciding how to develop an adjoining site. It is thus both a 'What have they been doing wrong and how can it be put right?' and a 'Which way should they go now?' case. Both the alternative development possibilities suggested appear to be attractive, but you needn't restrict yourself to them alone. In effect, we have presented you with a prime site, and it's up to you to decide what you want to do with it.

Evaluating the options will involve you in doing some of the calculations that you would normally expect to find done for you in a respectable feasibility study. As we said in the Introduction, this is a little artificial, but you may well have to do this kind of work yourself at some time.

Once again, you will see that we have located our imaginary hotel in a genuine town. The background data we have provided are genuine enough, but 'Southgate Street' does not exist, and no resemblance to any existing establishment is intended.

CASE STUDY

INTRODUCTION

The Dee Hall Hotel is owned by Duchy Hotels Ltd. The company was formed in the Autumn of 1982 by David Edwards (the owner of a successful building firm) and Eric Hughes (owner of a chain of five successful restaurants). The company currently owns and operates the following:

Hotel	Purchased	Rooms
Dee Hall, Chester	1983	84
Randolph, Preston	1983	30

The Dee Hall is the larger and more tourist-orientated of the two, with a substantial business clientele, and it remains the group's 'flagship'.

The Dee Hall was taken over from its previous owners by Duchy Hotels Ltd in June 1983 at a valuation of £2,000,000. The purchase price included the adjoining Dee Cinema. This was small and old-fashioned. It had been successful up to the 1960s, but had latterly declined to being used as a bingo hall. The then management of the Dee Hall, concerned about the effect that this increasingly seedy and dilapidated property was having on the hotel's image, bought it in 1982 with a view to subsequent development, but no action had been taken before the hotel was sold to Duchy. Duchy arranged for its demolition, and this was undertaken during 1984. The site, which has an area of approximately 5,000 square feet and is freehold, is currently vacant and boarded off. Duchy understand that the planning authorities would welcome its development along lines in keeping with the 'olde-worlde' atmosphere of Southgate Street.

Duchy have deferred development of the cinema site until they had established the strengths and weaknesses of the hotel and considered the commercial possibilities of the site.

Duchy Hotel's financial year ends on 31 October. The company's balance sheet and the Dee Hall's profit and loss account and other operating figures are provided below (pp. 79–85).

At the end of 1985 the directors met to consider these figures and to determine future development policy with regard to the Dee Hall, in particular what to do with the adjoining Dee Cinema site. In addition to the financial and statistical information already mentioned they had available two reports, one on Conferences, the other on Leisure Facilities in Hotels. These documents are also provided below (pp. 86–95).

CHESTER

Chester is well served by the transport system. The railway station is close to the city centre, and the motorway is nearby, giving rapid and easy access to Manchester, Liverpool and North Wales.

Population data for Chester are as follows:

	Actual	Forecast High	Forecast Low
1971	114,900	—	—
1981	116,300	—	—
1986	—	120,000	116,000
1994	—	121,500	118,000

These figures need to be considered within the context of Cheshire as a whole, which rose from 866,556 in 1971 to 926,293 in 1981. Chester is not a town in isolation but the focal point for a large area, and there is a large and increasing potential market.

The population's age structure is as follows:

Age	Number	%
0–15	25,360	21.8
16–44	47,160	40.5
45–64	26,690	23.0
65+	17,100	14.7

Economic indicators show that Cheshire claims to be one of the richest counties in the North of England, with hourly earnings considerably higher than the average for England as a whole. Car ownership levels in Cheshire are markedly above the British average. These facts support the contention that the market's purchasing power is high. Approximately 26 per cent of the male 'head of household' population are in socio-income groups 'A' or 'B', compared with 15.1 per cent for the rest of the United Kingdom.

Within Chester itself there is a significant amount of employment in the county administration, manufacturing and service industries, including over 7,000 employed in shops. These service up to 80,000 people, and their high quality acts as an attraction to tourists.

Chester has attracted tourists from an early date. In 1779 Boswell wrote: 'I was quite enchanted with Chester that I could with difficulty quit it.' The first guide-book to the city was published in 1781, and it has long been established as a compulsory item on the tourist itinerary for both foreigners (especially North Americans) and Britons. The attractions include the Roman walls, the castle, the cathedral, the racecourse, the zoo and the famous 'Rows' (shops set in a seventeenth- and eighteenth-century environment). Chester is said to draw more visitors than any city in England other than London and York. The total is well over 1,000,000 per year. People visit the city all year round, though the influx is at its highest in the summer. Weekend breaks have been particularly successful.

There are also many recreational facilities in Chester which draw local residents into the centre of the city. They cater for all interests: sporting, political, charitable, artistic and social. There are two theatres and a cinema, together with canal and boat clubs on the river. The Northgate Leisure Centre is one of the best in the North West.

The restaurants (especially those within the city walls) are generally packed at lunchtimes and busy in the evenings. The local planning authority's policy of maintaining a balance between commercial, administrative and service industries has meant that restaurants are in short supply. A substantial market exists for reasonably priced, good quality meals, available in an informal setting and which can be obtained and consumed within a fairly short time.

THE DEE HALL HOTEL

The Dee Hall is situated on Southgate Street, Chester, close to the South Gate itself. Beside and to the rear of it is a pedestrian precinct. The bedrooms on the south side overlook the Roman wall, the river and the countryside beyond; those on Southgate Street have a good view of the city's traditional black and white timbered shops, while the inner rooms overlook a pleasant and well-maintained courtyard and garden.

The hotel has 10 single bedrooms, 24 doubles and 50 twins. All the twin and double rooms have baths and toilets en suite, together with colour TVs and central heating. The single rooms also have TVs, but only washbasins in the rooms. They are served by 2 separate bathrooms and WCs.

The hotel's image is in keeping with the general style of buildings in the centre of Chester. The original frontage has been preserved intact, and though the side wings have been substantially rebuilt to permit the addition of a second floor, the overall style and character have been preserved. The reception area, restaurant and bar are furnished and decorated to conform to this image, conveying an image of quiet, old-fashioned comfort and luxury.

The hotel has no private parking space but has arranged concessionary access to a municipal multi-storey car park nearby off Southgate Street. Guests purchase £1 all-day tickets on registration, and these monies are remitted in full to the council. This arrangement has proved mutually satisfactory, and Duchy envisage no changes in the immediate future.

The restaurant, which is known as the Dee Room, is an attractive feature. It seats approximately 180 persons for full silver service, and has been redecorated by Duchy throughout in traditional English style.

The bars are on the ground floor and can be reached by separate entrances: the vault bar from the street and the lounge bar from the front of the hotel. They are linked by a glass partition door which may be opened if required. The vault bar seats approximately 55 persons and is more attractive to the younger drinkers because of its atmosphere and prices. The lounge bar looks out on the garden with two doors giving access to the terrace and seats some 100 persons. It is used mainly in the evening by guests dining in the restaurant. Both bars are serviced by a central servery through the lounge bar.

Duchy retained all the staff employed at the time of the takeover, with the exception of the previous General Manager, who preferred to retire. Duchy appointed Chris Winter as General Manager.

The Accommodation Department had an Accommodation Manager, a Head Receptionist, 2 full-time and 2 part-time Receptionists. Bookings procedures were based on a conventional chart with Whitney diary and room racks, while billing was based on Sweda machines.

The Head Housekeeper had 2 Assistant Housekeepers and a staff of 4–6 part-time Housekeeping Assistants depending on the season. Housekeeping operations were based on the linen room (where both linen and cleaning materials were stored) and there were still several twenty-year-old suction cleaners in use.

There was a Head Porter, 2 Assistant Porters and 2 Maintenance Men.

The restaurant and bar operations were under the control of the Food and Beverage Manager, who oversaw the activities of the Head Waiter, Chef and bar staff. Equipment was conventional but well maintained.

The pre-Duchy management had co-ordinated the hotel's activities through regular weekly meetings of senior staff (in practice the

Accommodation Manager, Head Receptionist, Housekeeper, Food and Beverage Manager, Head Chef and Head Waiter). These employees were competent and experienced. All except the House-keeper were male and all were British. The meetings provided an opportunity to exchange information about future events and to discuss problems of mutual interest. The meetings were informal and were not normally based upon consideration of specific statistical or financial reports, being instead discursive, impressionistic and somewhat gossipy.

The hotel had prided itself upon being 'a good employer'. It had always been generous in terms of sick pay and sympathetic and understanding towards employees with family problems, though it expected high standards of dress and deportment and lateness, absenteeism and incivility were not tolerated. The staff regarded the administration as 'firm but fair', and most seemed to appreciate what a younger and better educated workforce might have regarded as a somewhat paternalistic attitude. The hotel had not participated in any formal training scheme, nor accepted industrial release students, nor recruited graduates: the previous General Manager having held the view that the only worthwhile training was a lengthy apprenticeship within the industry.

Winter embarked upon a more systematic approach to the manpower function. He issued guidelines clarifying policies and procedures regarding recruitment, selection and promotions, and began to encourage staff to undertake further training, either through part-time/distance HCIMA or day-release City and Guilds courses. There was covert opposition to these measures from the older departmental heads, who displayed considerable ingenuity in discovering reasons why staff should not be released. They also resisted Winter's efforts to reduce labour costs both through the more efficient deployment of staff and the consideration of new technology.

Winter knew that three key departmental managers would be retiring between mid 1985 and 1987. The Food and Beverage Manager was the first to leave. His replacement was recruited from a major national hotel group and was a young hotel and catering graduate with five year's post-qualification experience. His brief was to improve the professionalism of the department's management, reduce costs and raise productivity. His style turned out to be somewhat autocratic and abrasive, and he was regarded with suspicion and some dislike by the older departmental managers.

The Restaurant Manager retired six months later, and was replaced by another outsider, this time a male HND diploma holder with eight years' experience in hotels and restaurants. Winter and the new Food and Beverage manager had considered that the best applicant was a female graduate with a proven record and innovative ideas, but there was opposition from the Head Chef and the rest of the 'old guard', who contacted the previous owner: he in turn had spoken to David Edwards, who had rung Winter and suggested 'cooling it' (the disappointed applicant had subsequently been taken on by Duchy's expanding Hotels Division).

Apart from the Head Chef, who is 53, opposition has come mainly from the Accommodation Manager, who is unqualified but very experienced: he believes that the old ways are the best ways and has generally received the support of his department heads, who owe their positions to him. The Head Receptionist has recently been showing signs of some disquiet, however: he has invested in a home computer and has been rather tentatively advocating the advantages of word processing and computerized accounting. The Head Housekeeper is due to retire in late 1986 and the Accommodation Manager at the end of 1987.

New management meetings have been established: the management team has been reduced to Winter plus the Food and Beverage and Accommodation Managers. These meetings are concerned with departmental performances, for which the managers are now directly accountable. A formal system of performance appraisal was introduced in late 1985: its first full run is due to take place in May 1986.

Winter has also tried to introduce a new system of joint consultation, but with disappointing results to date. His new Food and Beverage Manager appears to accept the idea as theoretically desirable, but gives it a low priority in practice: privately, he has been urging Winter to 'crack the whip a bit', arguing that the whole establishment needs 'a good shake up' before reforms can be introduced effectively.

Labour turnover has been increasing, especially in the accommodation department and (more recently) in the restaurant, with a disturbing 20 per cent rise in accidents in housekeeping and the restaurant.

With Winter's agreement the new Food and Beverage Manager started to take on industrial release students in 1985. Some were from a local technical college and were taken for short periods. In summer 1986 it is planned to take two HND or degree students: their training schemes provide for them to understudy intermediate departmental managers (including the Head Housekeeper) for six-week periods.

The previous management had relied upon the financial accounts as the main control mechanism, supplemented by weekly accommodation letting reports and an orthodox stock control system. The senior departmental heads were familiar with their systems and experienced in detecting and preventing errors, both deliberate and accidental.

Winter had wanted to introduce a budgetary control system based on monthly management accounts with the emphasis on key figures. His new Food and Beverage Manager is in favour, but the idea was resisted by the original departmental heads, who made it clear that they preferred the old system. Because of David Edwards' instruction to 'cool it', Winter did not insist on implementing his proposals in full. However, he has insisted on a better system of debtor management with a proper analysis of debtor accounts and a tighter credit policy, has required full explanations of any discounted room rates or complimentaries and has introduced spot checks to compare the Housekeeper's reports and Reception's daily letting reports. He has also rationalized the range of wine and spirits stocks to reduce the stockturn ratio, introduced purchasing specifications, tightened up on the ordering system, established a fixed asset register and got the Accommodation Manager to prepare a five-year rolling plan for plant and equipment maintenance, as well as tightening up on staff overtime and casual workers' pay.

Con Tours (the big London-based travel agents) have an arrangement with the hotel by which they receive preference bookings during June/July/August in exchange for an undertaking to take up a minimum number of bookings for the 'shoulder' months of May and September. This arrangement accounts for the bulk of the hotel's travel agent bookings. The proportion of rooms held back for this purpose is renegotiated annually: Winter has agreed to continue the 1985 arrangements over the following summer, i.e. 30 per cent over June–August and 15 per cent in May and September. Con Tours have requested an additional booking equivalent to one coach load of 46 sleepers for a two-night stay in each week in May–August. The hotel gives Con Tours a special price of 75 per cent of

DUCHY HOTELS LTD: FINANCIAL INFORMATION

Balance Sheet as at 31 October 1985

	Cost	Depreciation	1985 £(000) Net	1984 £(000)
Fixed assets:				
Land and buildings	3,000	200	2,800	2,900
Fixtures and fittings	280	20	260	260
	3,280	220	3,060	3,160
Cost of shares in group companies			500	500
Current assets:				
Stocks	140			125
Debtors	460			430
Cash	180	780		160
Less Current liabilities				
Creditors	410			450
Corporation tax	130			145
Proposed dividend	100	640		100
Net current assets			140	20
			3,700	3,680
Less Amounts falling due after more than 1 year:				
9% Debentures			200	180
			£3,500	£3,500
Financed by:				
Share capital, authorized and issued:				
3,000,000 £1 ordinary shares, fully paid			3,000	3,000
Reserves:				
General reserve			500	500
Shareholder's interest			£3,500	£3,500

THE DEE HALL HOTEL: FINANCIAL INFORMATION

Profit and Loss Accounts (Years Ended 31 October)

	1981 £	1982 £	1983 £	1984 £	1985 £
Room sales	501,380	493,392	522,504	530,997	585,197
Food sales	420,360	360,560	373,790	396,050	448,950
Beverage sales	210,110	203,190	208,980	222,020	228,030
Other sales	15,600	14,700	15,800	15,900	16,000
Total sales	1,147,450	1,071,842	1,121,074	1,164,967	1,278,177
Room profit	501,380	493,390	522,500	531,000	586,000
Food profit	210,770	180,210	187,500	192,000	261,000
Beverage profit	91,010	99,080	106,900	103,800	108,000
Other profit	10,200	8,010	8,500	8,600	9,000
Gross profit	813,360	780,690	825,400	835,400	964,000

Less:					
Wages	336,420	370,590	360,200	365,306	385,000
Property expenses:					
Maintenance	64,000	52,600	52,600	55,300	57,500
Depreciation	51,000	51,000	51,000	51,000	53,000
Rates etc.	21,000	22,000	23,000	24,000	24,500
Operating expenses:					
Heat/light	35,000	36,000	36,800	38,100	41,000
Administration	45,000	45,700	45,700	46,800	48,000
Marketing	15,600	16,000	18,100	20,200	22,000
Sundries	5,700	7,700	6,000	7,000	8,000
Net profit	£239,640	£179,100	£232,000	£227,694	£325,000

Food and Beverage Departmental Results (Years Ended 31 October)

	1983		1984		1985	
	£	£	£	£	£	£
Food						
Breakfast	93,475		97,504		105,497	
Lunch	76,972		82,524		87,001	
Dinner	188,446		199,012		232,947	
Bar snacks	14,897		17,010		23,505	
	373,790		396,050		448,950	
Food costs	186,290		204,050		187,950	
Gross profit		187,500		192,000		261,000
Beverages						
Lunch	9,187		11,903		12,502	
Dinner	71,795		72,004		60,302	
Lounge bar	76,995		80,009		83,012	
Vault bar	51,003		58,104		72,214	
	208,980		222,020		228,030	
Less Beverage costs	102,080		118,220		120,030	
Gross profit		106,900		103,800		108,000
Total gross profit		294,400		295,800		369,000
Less Wages		174,000		176,000		188,000
Operating expenses		116,600		121,200		127,000
Net operating profit		£3,800		£(1,400)		£54,000

Monthly Food and Beverages Sales Analysis

	Food 1983 £	1984 £	1985 £	Beverages 1983 £	1984 £	1985 £
July	44,050	46,240	49,560	20,140	22,100	22,820
August	42,330	44,780	48,990	25,750	25,840	27,040
September	31,990	35,870	41,470	14,900	16,310	16,030
October	30,020	31,350	34,850	13,240	13,980	13,650
November	27,080	27,000	34,460	12,690	13,870	14,220
December	43,000	45,590	49,060	23,450	25,050	26,470
January	20,080	20,000	25,750	15,040	16,350	16,850
February	19,790	20,780	25,890	11,850	12,680	13,410
March	22,230	23,420	27,310	15,120	15,240	15,780
April	24,740	26,000	28,430	15,230	16,580	15,760
May	30,660	33,020	37,000	17,720	19,890	21,050
June	38,000	42,000	46,180	23,830	24,130	24,950
Totals	£373,970	£396,050	£448,950	£208,980	£222,020	£228,030

Monthly Accommodation Revenues

	1981 £	1982 £	1983 £	1984 £	1985 £
July	57,014	56,406	58,260	59,338	62,488
August	56,381	55,917	58,427	59,160	62,048
September	44,803	54,198	58,420	58,911	62,003
October	36,096	37,056	39,225	40,287	48,010
November	36,187	32,013	35,893	36,704	35,190
December	36,252	35,557	37,803	38,599	49,997
January	34,143	30,111	32,600	33,104	34,021
February	35,240	30,404	33,089	34,052	36,187
March	33,796	32,699	34,903	34,093	36,707
April	36,104	32,401	32,678	34,804	40,094
May	38,947	40,512	42,405	43,095	56,255
June	56,417	56,118	58,801	58,850	62,197
Totals	£501,380	£493,392	£522,504	£530,997	£585,197

Monthly Room Sales

	1981 No.	1982 No.	1983 No.	1984 No.	1985 No.
July	2,432	2,492	2,480	2,468	2,496
August	2,374	2,409	2,488	2,420	2,479
September	1,987	2,378	2,430	2,463	2,471
October	1,630	1,794	1,785	1,857	1,923
November	1,636	1,482	1,381	1,372	1,416
December	1,604	1,679	1,721	1,780	1,918
January	1,520	1,380	1,420	1,362	1,421
February	1,640	1,481	1,430	1,421	1,536
March	1,618	1,579	1,532	1,507	1,553
April	1,790	1,610	1,609	1,592	1,618
May	1,809	1,988	2,197	2,058	2,255
June	2,360	2,470	2,458	2,479	2,483
Totals	22,400	22,742	22,931	22,779	23,569

Sources of Accommodation Demand

	1981		1982		1983		1984		1985	
	S %	W %	S %	W %	S %	W %	S %	W %	S %	W %
Direct	54	38	43	36	39	33	37	32	34	29
Travel agent	10	2	24	8	31	17	34	18	40	22
Company	34	54	30	50	29	43	28	42	25	40
Chance	2	6	3	6	1	7	1	8	1	9
Totals	100	100	100	100	100	100	100	100	100	100

S = Summer, W = Winter

Analysis of Guests by Country of Origin

	1981 %	1982 %	1983 %	1984 %	1985 %
UK	72	80	82	82	76
USA	16	10	9	8	12
Other	12	10	9	10	12
Totals	100	100	100	100	100

the standard room and table d'hôte rates (plus, of course, a complimentary room for the guide/courier). However, group tour visitors do not order à la carte items and consume fewer drinks with or after their meals. The group tour contract also means that a mixture of market segments is using the hotel during the summer. One or two of the hotel's regular visitors and local residents who use the hotel frequently have told Winter privately that they think it is a mistake and that it is leading to friction and a lowering of standards.

FEASIBILITY REPORT ON CONFERENCE TRADE IN CHESTER

Presented to: The Manager
                Dee Hall Hotel
                Southgate Street
                Chester

Introduction

The aim of this report is to evaluate the potential of the Dee Hall, Chester, as a Conference Centre. It takes as its basis the British Tourist Authority's 1977 definition of a conference, i.e.:

- A meeting in hired premises

- Lasting a minimum of 6 hours

- Attended by a minimum of 25 persons

- Having a fixed agenda or programme.

Part 1: Hotels and Conferences

Although 24 large conference complexes have been built since 1975 and 22 new centres are expected within the next five years, hotels are still well placed to cater for conference business, as shown by the following table:

Venue	1977	1978	1979	1980
In municipal centres	213	424	333	349
% change per annum		+99%	−22%	+5%
In hotels	N/A	3,158	3,598	3,977
% change per annum			+14%	+11%
In educational centres	N/A	493	622	695
% change per annum			+26%	+12%
Total conferences	3,796	4,075	4,553	5,021
% change per annum		+7%	+12%	+10%

Source: Lawson, I. R. *Conference, Convention and Exhibition Facilities: A Handbook of Planning, Design and Management* (London: Architectural Press, 1981).

In general, hotels cater for the medium-sized business conference, as shown by the following table:

Venue	Type of business	Average length	Average number of delegates
Conference centre	International/ corporate users	1–3 days	200–400
Hotels	Business	67% 1 day	50
	Trade associations	20% 2 days	
	Professional/ social groups	13% +2 days	
Universities	Academic/cultural	4.5 days	120

Source: Lawson (1981).

A 1979 survey of 1,678 hotels covering almost all the UK hotels offering such facilities revealed that the average hotel of 81 rooms provided the following facilities:

Facility	Area		Seating
	Metres²	Feet²	
Main hall	207	2,230	192
Supplementary Meeting rooms	137	1,470	127

Source: Lawson (1981).

Trends in Demand

It is generally agreed that the conference market is growing by approximately 10 per cent per annum. The main factors leading to this increase in demand for conferences are:

- An increase in the number of multinational companies

- The development of co-operatives, professional associations and pressure groups

- The increasing need for communication at a personalized level

- The need for updating regarding information and techniques

- The increasing need for co-ordination

- The relative ease of travel

- An increase in per capita income

- Rising educational standards

- Changes in sales techniques (e.g. co-ordinated product launches)

● An increase in specialized training.

A survey by Spectrum Communication Group showed that 70 per cent of the companies questioned intended to increase their budget allocation to conferences for 1985/86, whereas only 19 per cent estimated that their budgets would be decreased. The same survey showed that the majority of meetings would fall into the 100–280 delegate bracket, and that provincial hotels would be the greatest beneficiaries. The trend is now towards small regional events, due largely to a reduction in the funds available for overnight accommodation and travel.

Part 2: Criteria Involved in Conference Venue Selection
Lawson (1981) identifies several factors which influence the selection of a conference venue:

1. *Attractiveness* of the location to delegates and their accompanying guests

2. *Accessibility* – the ease of travel and its costs

3. *Equipment* – the availability of conference-related equipment and support services such as catering

4. *Rotational needs* – the venue may change when meetings are held regularly to allow delegates equal ease of access

5. *Dates* to coincide with other related events in the area to attract attendance, or to avoid unrelated events which might distract delegates.

We carried out a survey to determine how buyers of conference facilities selected venues. Questionnaires were sent to 400 conference-holding organizations in the UK, of whom 205 responded. A summary of their findings is presented below:

(a) Respondents indicated that:

● 95% used conference facilities at least once a year
● 60% said the length of a meeting was usually 1 day
● 40% said the length of a meeting was more than 1 day

Time preferences were:

Weekdays	69%
Weekends	6%
Both	25%
	100%

(b) Respondents were asked to assign scores to the factors influencing choice of venue in terms of general area (1 point for the highest importance, 5 for the lowest). The results were as follows:

1.	Accessibility	144 points
2.	Conference facilities	149 points
3.	Area attractiveness	254 points
4.	Entertainment	302 points

(c) Respondents were asked how far they were prepared to travel for a conference:

Up to 100 miles	46%
Up to 200 miles	35%
Abroad	19%
	100%

(d) Respondents were asked to indicate the relative importance of factors determining the choice of the specific conference centre/hotel as opposed to the general venue (1 point for the highest importance, 5 for the lowest). The results were as follows:

1.	Conference facilities	152 points
2.	Price	178 points
3.	Size of conference centre	194 points
4.	Availability of hotel accommodation	231 points

Additional factors mentioned (in order of significance) included (i) cleanliness, (ii) separate conference rooms, (iii) accommodation for delegates in the same building, (iv) good parking facilities, (v) smart, impressive hotel/centre, (vi) booking fee discounts for large numbers, (vii) late opening bars, (viii) all single rooms.

(e) Respondents were asked to indicate their requirements for catering facilities. The results were as follows:

Evening:	A la carte menu	19%	Lunch:	Buffet	65%
	Fixed menu	72%		Light snack	17%
Tea/coffee		71%			

Part 3: Analysis of Conference Trade in Chester

There is no major conference centre in Chester. Of the local hotels 11 have conference facilities. Nevertheless, we were unable to book a proposed two-day conference for 70 delegates within the next three months.

Our inquiries revealed the following:

(a) Approximately 50 per cent of conference delegates/officials require an overnight stay.

(b) 80 per cent of all delegates have a hotel lunch and all had refreshments during the day in the form of tea and/or coffee.

(c) Hotels involved in the conference trade are also engaged in 'function' trade, particularly at weekends, and many are fully booked for two months ahead.

(d) The current day conference rate per delegate in the Chester area is approximately £12. This covers room and equipment hire, consumables (e.g. flip charts), coffee, biscuits, lunch, tea and biscuits and is inclusive of VAT.

(e) The average overnight rate per delegate in the Chester area is £30. This covers the conference charges detailed in (d) above plus accommodation and table d'hôte evening meal. Conference organizer(s) are normally given complimentary status: the accepted ratio is approximately 1 organizer per 50 delegates.

We carried out a survey to determine how Chester was perceived as a venue for conferences as compared with other towns in the North and Midlands.

The images of 20 towns and cities were measured on 12 dimensions that had emerged as relevant during preliminary work. A standard method of collecting image data was used: i.e. respondents were presented with a card listing 20 towns and cities which they then scored as interviewers read out 12 pairs of statements, each representing the positive and negative sides of an image dimension.

It is gratifying to report that Chester ranked second only to Manchester as a suitable place to hold a medium-sized conference.

CONCLUSIONS

The English Tourist Board forecast is for 10 per cent growth in conference spending over the next two years.

Chester is a very attractive tourist town which has a desirable 'image' both nationally and internationally.

Although Chester has several establishments already catering for the conference trade, the indications are that there is still significant undercapacity. There appear to be no major new competitive developments being planned. Given the attractiveness of the venue, this undercapacity can be expected to continue in the medium term.

We believe that there is still room for the hotel to expand into the market for 30–90 delegate conferences in the Chester area and recommend, therefore, that consideration be given to developing the Dee Hall as a conference site.

FEASIBILITY REPORT ON LEISURE CENTRES IN HOTELS

Presented to: The Manager
Dee Hall Hotel
Southgate Street
Chester

Introduction
During this century the time available for leisure (defined as time spent not at work) has increased significantly due to long annual holidays and a change from a six-day to a five-day working week. It is expected that this trend will continue, with further reductions in the number of hours worked and more people taking early retirement. Experts say there has never been so much free time available to so many people. This has led to a marked growth in active recreation.

Health and fitness now equal big business. Henley Forecasting believe that interest in sports activity will experience positive growth over the next few years in response to a rise in income levels and an increasing awareness of the importance of regular exercise in maintaining good health. They assess the growth of the health and leisure market as follows:

	1980	1982	1984	1986	1988	1990
Sports goods (£m)	783	845	1,029	1,227	1,451	1,725
Sports clothing (£m)	612	770	988	1,115	1,307	1,549

91

The health and fitness revolution originated in the USA, where 49 per cent of the population now exercise regularly. Such a figure is likely to be reproduced in the UK in the near future.

The actual leisure product ranges from clubs offering relaxation and body conditioning facilities to those geared to developing high levels of physical fitness through training programmes. The more general facilities (such as swimming pools, saunas and basic gymnasiums) have a wide range of appeal, attracting families and individuals alike.

Membership of leisure clubs is on the increase due to a growing demand for professional instruction in keeping fit. There are positive implications for the providers of well organized clubs offering guidance and instruction at varying levels.

Leisure and Hotels
The hotel industry is responding to current trends with the development of leisure and fitness centres in a great many hotels.

Hotels are expected to spend in excess of £30m in 1986 on adding leisure facilities to their properties and creating 300 new jobs within this specialist area. The hotel industry is responding to the leisure boom with developments taking place at both large and small establishments in the United Kingdom. All the big groups approached by the magazine *Hospitality* had big leisure plans in the pipeline. Smaller hotel groups are also currently involved in leisure centre development, as are many independent hotels.

Leisure and the Regular Market
It is clear that this increase of interest in health and fitness is becoming increasingly important in determining the choice of hotel. Research carried out in 1985 showed that 20–25 per cent of hotel guests cared sufficiently about fitness to view the provision of leisure facilities as a major determinant in selecting a place to stay (*Lodging Hospitality*, Feb. 1985). An in-house survey at one establishment found that 48 per cent of business guests went to the hotel because they wanted to use its leisure facilities.

One group offer guests comprehensive fitness tests in some of their properties. The results are used to devise an exercise programme which the individual is encouraged to follow. Regular travellers committed to such programmes are likely to choose hotels providing appropriate health and fitness facilities. This is likely to encourage loyalty to the chain.

Leisure and the Weekend Market

The growth of the leisure industry is coupled with a growing trend towards spending weekends away from home relaxing in a leisure environment. This has stimulated hotel interest in the development of leisure centres. The in-house survey referred to above found that 78 per cent of the weekend guests had gone to the hotel because they had read it offered leisure facilities.

It is clear that a leisure centre can turn a Monday-to-Thursday out-of-town operation into a seven-day-a-week one and thus substantially increase occupancy rates.

It need hardly be pointed out that the provision of additional health/leisure facilities would also justify an increase in room rates.

Leisure and the Conference Market

Many hoteliers believe that leisure facilities give them the edge over their competitors in relation to conference business. We can quote one as saying 'We see it as giving a distinctive edge to our marketing image amongst a predominantly business clientele.'

Another group offer full fitness tests in some of their properties. The results of these are used to devise an exercise programme for the individual to follow. Encouraged to follow such a programme, those who travel a lot are more likely to choose hotels providing appropriate health and fitness facilities. This is likely to encourage loyalty to the chain.

We have surveyed 176 companies who hold regular conferences in order to find out how highly they rated leisure facilities in deciding on their choice of venue. The results were as follows:

Very important	8.5%
Important	19.3%
Average importance	29.0%

Thus over half of the respondents gave consideration to the availability of leisure facilities. These results suggest that hotels providing such facilities are likely to have a competitive edge when it comes to the choice of conference venue.

Local Demand

Local (i.e. non-resident) demand for leisure facilities is difficult to quantify but clearly could be an important source of revenue. Such demand could come from local business and professional groups. Normal practice is to offer club membership. This provides regular income from subscriptions and offers a means of restricting usage if necessary. Temporary club membership can be offered to hotel guests as part of the total accommodation package.

Costs

A leisure facility at a hotel represents a substantial investment. Costs vary from establishment to establishment, but are generally between £250,000 and £500,000. One large group has found that a typical leisure club with heated indoor swimming pool, spa bath, sauna, solarium, steam room, massage area and multi-gym costs about £350,000 to construct and equip.

Running costs for a facility of this type are as follows:

	£
Staffing	10,000
Heating/maintenance	5,000
Laundry/water rates	5,000

Allowance would also have to be made for depreciation (estimates of equipment life vary, but 10 years is a reasonable average) and interest on capital.

Revenues

The factors to be taken into account are as follows:

1. *Increased occupancy rates.* We suggest that this might conservatively be estimated at 5 per cent in the case of the Dee Hall.

2. *Increased room rates.* Comparisons suggest that for comparable hotels rack rates can be increased by an average of £5 per night.

3. *Income from local business/professional/resident members.* Again, comparisons with comparable hotels suggest that this might amount to 250 day-time members each paying c. £300 per annum.

4. *Additional profits* from increased sales of food/drink to:

   (a) extra residents
   (b) local members.

   Experience to date suggests that the latter group are likely to average 1 visit per week with an ASP of £2.50.

Conclusions

Hotel leisure facilities have been shown to be a worthwhile investment in that they can:

1. Attract business guests

2. Increase weekend occupancy

3. Attract conference business

4. Create additional revenue from membership fees

5. Create additional food and beverage sales.

Even though many hoteliers admit that hotel guests are not always the principal users of leisure facilities, it has been shown that their existence does influence many people in their choice of a place to stay.

This market can be expected to grow since increased leisure time and rising disposable incomes are likely to lead to an increased take up of leisure activities.

PLANS

The Dee Hall Hotel – sketch view of cinema and hotel from Southgate Street.

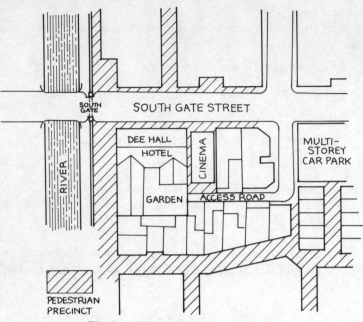

The Dee Hall Hotel – street location.

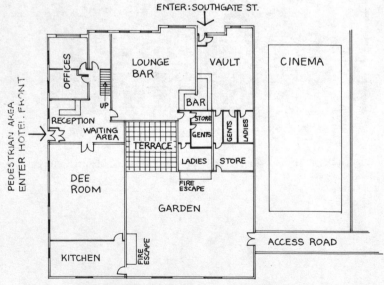

The Dee Hall Hotel – plan at ground level.

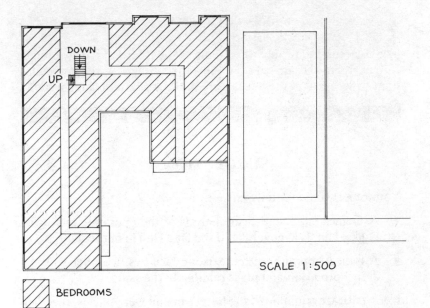

The Dee Hall Hotel – plan at first floor level (bedroom level 1).

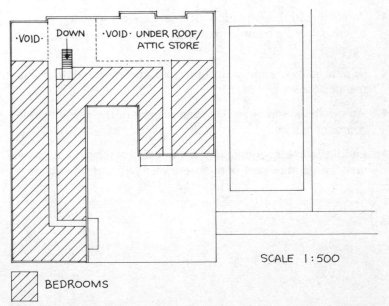

The Dee Hall Hotel – plan at second floor level (bedroom level 2).

INSTRUCTIONS

You are required to submit a report to the Board of Duchy Hotels Ltd, analysing the current situation and offering your recommendations with regard to the development of the adjacent cinema site.

SUGGESTIONS

Your report could usefully include:

- A financial and statistical analysis of the operating figures of Duchy Hotels in general and the Dee Hall in particular

- A critical appraisal of the existing facilities, together with re-design proposals and plans relating to the same

- A critical evaluation of the hotel's manpower policies, together with recommendations regarding future policy

- A critical review of general management procedures, with particular reference to the control systems operated to date

- A comparative evaluation of the two consultancy reports, coupled with a recommendation as to which (if either) should be adopted

- Capital financing and budget proposals in respect of the recommended course of action

- An outline marketing scheme in respect of the recommended course of action

- Outline building, equipment, staffing and management recommendations in respect of the recommended course of action.

CHAPTER 7

THE SUTTON MANOR CASE

You will have noticed in the last case that Duchy Hotels owned another, smaller hotel as well as the Dee Hall. Like other groups, they are likely to be interested in expansion, and can be expected to take an interest whenever there is a possibility of another hotel coming onto the market.

One of the problems they face, however, is that hotels have a relatively long pay-back period. If you try working out the return on a single room, using the well-known 1:1,000 room rate:room cost ratio, assuming a realistic annual occupancy rate (say 65 per cent) and providing for interest and tax, you will realize that it could take several decades to recover the original cost. Even allowing for inflation will not bring this down to less than twenty years.

This is one reason why there was a growing interest in timeshare in the late 1970s and early 1980s, and our next case is centred around this. Since you may well be as unfamiliar with the basic concepts as Duchy's two directors were, we have followed them through the preliminary learning process. However, we have stopped short at the implementation stage. There are still a lot of decisions to be taken before a successful timeshare operation can be 'got off the ground', and the real challenge in this case is to work out what these are.

CASE STUDY

INTRODUCTION

As noted in the previous case, Duchy Hotels Ltd was formed in the autumn of 1982 by David Edwards (the owner of a successful building firm) and Eric Hughes (owner of a chain of five successful restaurants). The company currently owns and operates the following:

Hotel	Purchased	Rooms
Dee Hall, Chester	1983	84
Randolph, Preston	1983	30

In April 1985, David Edwards learned through informal channels that there was a possibility of purchasing the Sutton Manor, an independent Lake District hotel owned and managed by James Edgar. He travelled up to Windermere to view the property and had exploratory discussions with Edgar, who indicated that he wished to retire but preferred to sell his hotel to an individual or small group rather than a national chain.

On his return, Edwards and his co-director Eric Hughes had a discussion.

———

EDWARDS: I've been having a look at a twenty-bed hotel up near Windermere. It could be on the market in the next month or so.

HUGHES: That's a bit outside our territory, isn't it?

EDWARDS: Not really. It's only an hour and a half up the M6.

HUGHES: Well, yes, but in that area it will be catering mainly for tourists, won't it?

EDWARDS: So does the Dee Hall. Anyhow, let me tell you what I've got in mind. I take it you're agreed that we ought to go on expanding our hotel interests, right?

HUGHES: Yes.

EDWARDS: And you'll agree that we're not doing that as quickly as we'd hoped?

HUGHES: I suppose so.

EDWARDS: Why is that?

HUGHES: You know perfectly well why not. We can't free enough capital to buy new sites *and* develop the earlier ones as we'd like. I mean, there's that cinema site at the Dee Hall for a start . . .

EDWARDS: Right. Well, I've been hearing quite a lot about time-share recently. You know the idea, don't you?

HUGHES: Only very vaguely. Isn't it for people who want holiday homes?

EDWARDS: Yes, but there are quite a few partly or wholly centred around hotels.

HUGHES: How does it work?

EDWARDS: Well, it starts with a developer. He either buys an existing property or builds a new one. Then he sells off 'timeshares', which is the right to occupy a unit for a fixed period every year. The period is usually a week, but all kinds of variations are possible.

HUGHES: What rights do purchasers have?

EDWARDS: The same as any other property owners. They can sell their timeshares, or rent them out, or even leave them to their heirs in their wills. The great advantage over owning a holiday home in the normal way is that the buyer only pays for one week instead of fifty-two.

HUGHES: Yes, but what about maintenance?

EDWARDS: The purchasers usually form an owners' association and subcontract that to a management company. This looks after the maintenance and levies an annual charge which is divided among the owners proportionately. As far as they are concerned it's a great deal cheaper than trying to maintain individual properties.

HUGHES: Yes, I can see that. But would people really want to spend all their holidays in the same place?

EDWARDS: A surprising number do, you know, especially if the place is as attractive as the Lake District. However, timeshare doesn't have to mean that. There are exchange schemes which allow owners to 'swop' their periods with comparable ones in other parts of the world.

HUGHES: All right. What's in it for the developer?

EDWARDS: Ah, that's the interesting bit. He gets his money back as soon as all the units are sold. I'm told that unit sales should normally yield about three times the building costs, and that he gets this back within three to five years.

HUGHES: Maybe. But how much does it cost to *sell* the units?

EDWARDS: Well, that *is* expensive. I'm told it usually costs about as much as the building costs. All the same, that still leaves around 33 per cent profit . . .

HUGHES: Mmmm . . . It's still a pretty new and unfamiliar business as far as we're concerned.

EDWARDS: Not entirely. You know quite a bit about speculative building, after all, and we both know something about hotels. Don't forget that timeshare hotels have to have restaurants, kitchens, bars and the like, so that the operating techniques aren't really very different. They need better leisure facilities, certainly, but given current trends that's a market we ought to be considering anyway.

HUGHES: I take it the developer usually acts as the management company?

EDWARDS: Yes, that's the norm. And don't forget that if it's a hotel based development he can go on letting his unsold units in the normal way.

HUGHES: I suppose he could even let units on behalf of owners, on an agency basis of course . . .

EDWARDS: Yes, indeed. You're beginning to see the possibilities.

HUGHES: Mmmm . . . So what you're suggesting is . . .?

EDWARDS: That we ought to have a careful look at the possibility of developing this hotel on a timeshare basis. If things went well, we'd get our investment back in five years, with a handsome profit as well, *and* we'd still have effective control of a hotel which we could continue to operate as part of our group. We'd also gain experience in a new and exciting sector. Even if things didn't go to plan, we'd still have a useful resort property . . .

HUGHES: Interesting . . . It needs a lot more work, though.

EDWARDS: Of course. But do you agree that we ought at least to carry out some preliminary studies?

HUGHES: Well, yes, I suppose so.

———

To: David Edwards

From: Eric Hughes

Date: 6 May 1985

Re: Timeshare owners' survey

I have managed to obtain a copy of a survey carried out by final year students from Manchester Polytechnic in 1984. Its conclusions were as follows:

Respondents had learned about timeshare from the following sources:

		%
Travel agents		5
Invitations to attend seminars		15
Advertisements:		
Newspapers	25	
Magazines	20	
Direct mail	5	50

Recommendations from owners   15%
Business connections   10
Other sources   5

                                  100

In every case, the purchaser had visited and stayed at the site before buying.

A timeshare development in a resort area needs to have sufficient facilities to attract visitors all the year round. It should provide:

1. An acceptable mix of accommodation facilities, namely, single, twin and three-bedded units plus 'studios'.

2. Catering facilities within the units.

3. An appropriate style of layout, furnishings and equipment for the accommodation units and public areas.

4. A range of indoor leisure facilities to enable owners to occupy themselves when the weather makes it necessary to stay 'on site'.

5. Alternative leisure facilities for the wives of golfers, hill climbers, etc.

6. Conference facilities to encourage company ownership.

7. Facilities to attract local residents so as to maximize usage of services and facilities.

The survey showed that the buyers attach considerable importance to the overall atmosphere created by the social amenities and the quality of the structures. Women were particularly influenced by the kitchen design.

Every respondent expected to receive psychological benefits related to:

1. Comfort, relaxation and a peaceful atmosphere.

2. Status through belonging to a group.

3. Possessing something different which they could talk to other people about.

Physical features were rated on a preference scale. The results were as follows (highest ranking first):

	Ranking
Site location and atmosphere	1
Quality of unit	2
Provision of indoor swimming pool	3
Cost of unit	4
Restaurant/bar availability	5
Exchange scheme membership	6
Boating and golfing facilities	7
Squash and tennis facilities	8
Gymnasium	9
Provision for children (e.g. a games room)	10
Inflation-proof holidays	11

This gives us a basis on which to plan.

———

To: Eric Hughes

From: David Edwards

Date: 8 May 1985

Re: Timeshare financing

Following our discussions, I have been looking into the financial aspects of the timeshare proposal.

1. The capital cost of the project would have to allow for:

    (a) The Sutton Manor's purchase price.

    (b) The cost of any necessary alterations and additions.

    (c) Any legal costs involved in setting up a timeshare scheme.

2. We would need to allow for the following expenses:

    (a) *Tax*. Apart from the obvious tax charge on company profits, it appears that VAT must be levied on the sale of usage of holiday accommodation such as houses, flats, chalets, etc., whether the accommodation is sold freehold, by lease or licence, or by club membership (in this last case VAT is levied on the joining fee). This does not apply to private owners selling their timeshares as long as this is not in furtherance of a trade or business.

(b) *Interest.* Clearly, we would need to allow for interest on any amounts borrowed to finance the development. It would be prudent to allow *c*. 12 per cent for this purpose.

(c) Our own obligation in respect of maintenance on unsold periods.

3. It seems to be agreed that the developer can expect to sell the units within a relatively short period, five years being a frequently quoted figure. This means that we should be able to approach sources of short- to medium-term finance rather than longer-term lenders, thus widening our options. I understand that the clearing banks are now involved with several developments, not only through providing loans, but also by acting as trustees.

Practically all of the capital outlay on building costs etc. needs to be incurred at the start (we have to have 'show' units and functioning leisure facilities in order to sell at all). I would assume that the marketing costs could be spread fairly evenly over the full five-year period. However, sales are likely to be slow at first. I have heard that the experience of a successful comparable venture was approximately as follows:

Year 1 sales	10% of total
Year 2 sales	15% of total
Year 3 sales	20% of total
Year 4 sales	25% of total
Year 5 sales	30% of total

Obviously a successful development generates a momentum of its own.

4. The tricky question would be the unit pricing structure. We can calculate the price per unit along the following lines:

$$\frac{\text{Development costs} + \text{Marketing costs} + \text{Required profit}}{\text{Total no. of units}}$$

However, this only yields an *average* selling price. Some units may have better locations or facilities than others, and it would be essential to reflect seasonality. After all, demand for July and August periods is likely to be much higher than that for November or February ones.

105

5. There are certain supplementary sources of revenue which might help to offset some of the costs. As you indicated, it ought to be possible to let unsold units in the normal way, and even to let owners' units on an agency basis. I have heard it suggested that there is some danger that prospective buyers might be put off by the idea that their units have been used in this way. However, it is part of the nature of timeshare that units will be used by other people, so I don't think this is very significant.

There are additional advantages in setting up a timeshare development in conjunction with an existing hotel. Buyers will almost certainly use the restaurant and bar, together with whatever leisure facilities are available, and a certain number will want bedrooms occasionally for 'overflow' guests. This might have a significant effect on out-of-season trade. At the same time, the hotel staff could also provide services on behalf of the maintenance company. They could deal with the cleaning and laundry, for instance, and handle bookings, as well as general maintenance.

In the long term, some of the earlier buyers will want to sell their timeshares, and the management company may undertake to do this for them on an agency basis, thus earning additional commission. This is not likely to be a significant item for the first five years or so, and we would of course have to give priority to selling our own unsold units first.

6. Some intending buyers might have difficulty in finding the purchase price. It would obviously be possible to provide some kind of assistance here. We might try to operate a deferred payments scheme ourselves. Alternatively, we could earn commission by putting such buyers in touch with a suitable finance house.

7. We also need to allow for insurance cover. The obvious risks are the usual ones of fire, flood, burglary, occupier's and employer's liability. Some of the cost can be borne by the management company and passed on to the owners through the maintenance charge, but the proportion relating to the construction and pre-sales periods will have to be borne by ourselves as developers. A further point is that I have been strongly advised that we should take out cover against the need to indemnify owners against not being able to occupy their units due to events such as fire, flood or damage by previous occu-

pants. These are not strictly speaking our responsibility, either as developers or as the management company, but the provision of such cover is a useful selling point. It ought to cover the cost of an equivalent holiday elsewhere.

———

To: David Edwards

From: Eric Hughes

Date: 14 May 1985

Re: Timeshare marketing

Timeshare is still a relatively new concept in this country. The first development was only founded in the mid 1970s, but there are now well over twenty in England, with another seven or eight in Scotland and two or three in Wales. Of course, that is still small stuff compared with developments elsewhere. There are over 600 in North America, about 50 in Mexico, 35 in the Caribbean, 200 in Europe, plus quite a few others scattered around in various holiday areas. Not bad going when you consider that there were only about 15–20 in all in 1975!

Nevertheless, it is still necessary to sell the 'idea' of timeshare before we can sell the units themselves. We must therefore give a lot of thought to publicity. I understand that advertisements in the 'property' or 'holiday' pages do not bring much of a response, and the best results are achieved by separate advertisements in an editorial page. We need to investigate this thoroughly.

Word of mouth is regarded as the best kind of advertising. It has been found elsewhere that once a development has become established, the second 50 per cent of all the time periods is largely sold through existing owners recommending the development to their friends. One successful American developer sold practically all his second phase units in this way before he actually put them onto the market.

Initially, however, an intensive marketing effort will be required. After all, we will be trying to sell each unit fifty times over rather than just once, as with the normal holiday home. We will have to arrange for advance publicity, set up an office and make arrangements to show prospective buyers around.

All this will cost money. I mentioned earlier that American experience suggests that marketing costs can be expected to equal the actual building costs of the unit, and we ought to regard this as the minimum outlay for planning purposes.

We need to identify the target market. The package would seem to be designed to appeal to people with enough money to make a 'once for all' holiday payment, but not enough to buy their own holiday home. A second and possibly overlapping category might be those who want to be free from the worries of maintaining such a holiday home. Obviously, the market must be prepared to consider taking a high proportion of their future holidays in the Lake District.

It is essential to belong to a major exchange organization, because buyers do not wish to be tied to taking their holidays in the same area year after year. These organizations protect their subscribers by laying down high standards, and membership acts as an indication to prospective buyers that the development has attained those standards. They are financed by annual site fees (paid by the developers) and annual membership fees (these are paid by the owners, though it is common for developers to offer free membership for a year or more, depending on the number of weeks purchased). Obviously, exchanges are restricted in terms of the type of unit and period: in principle owners can only exchange between similar classes of unit and periods, though they can usually 'trade down' into smaller units or less attractive periods.

I gather that on average owners take two holidays in their own unit for every one arranged through an exchange scheme. In fact, research in North America and Europe has shown that many buyers never actually use their own timeshare accommodation themselves but do use it for exchange purposes: this kind of owner normally buys a timeshare unit close to his own main residence.

We shouldn't ignore this as a possible selling line. One approach used in the USA is to market the units as 'retreats' for busy managers. It has been found there that a high proportion of buyers actually live within 50 miles of the timeshare development and use it to relax completely for one week per year. Obviously there is a useful potential market in the North of England.

One other important possible market might be companies. Quite a few companies purchase units. They use them for meetings, especially the 'let's get away from it all' kind. They can let successful managers use them as a kind of bonus or incentive. They can also use them to accommodate overseas staff home on leave, or to entertain business associates, or even as retirement gifts for long service staff.

I attach some background data relevant to the proposal:

**Total consumer expenditure on hotels and catering
in real terms (1980 = 100):**

	Hotels and guest houses	Restaurants and snack bars	Pubs and clubs	Total
1979	102.0	107.6	106.0	104.0
1980	100.0	100.0	100.0	100.0
1981	96.8	94.2	93.8	90.0
1982	95.2	95.7	91.3	90.2
1983	98.4	95.2	91.5	91.0

(Source: HCITB–MMD Consultants Ltd)

Consumer spending trends 1974–82:

	Per year
Catering and accommodation	−0.5%
Other leisure activities	+2.3%
Beer	−0.5%
On-licence sales	−1.1%
Off-licence sales	+5.5%

(Source: HCITB–MMD Consultants Ltd)

Holiday accommodation trends 1965–81:

Accommodation used (%)	1965	1975	1981
Serviced (hotel, etc.)	45	36	27
Self-catering	24	36	47
Friends/relatives	24	21	22
Other	7	7	4
Totals	100	100	100

(Source: Tourist Boards)

To: Eric Hughes

From: David Edwards

Date: 21 May 1985

Re: Legal aspects of timeshare

I have been talking with our legal adviser about these. He made
the following points:

1. Ownership

Apart from charities, only a maximum of four people can hold the legal title to freehold or leasehold property in England. In order to allow timeshare owners to exercise property rights, therefore, it is essential to form either a limited company or a club.

If the developer owns the land, he can either grant a long-term lease at a nominal rent to a management company, or else transfer the freehold to the management company. In either case the management company may proceed to:

(a) Grant long-term fixed annual holiday occupation rights to buyers;

(b) Make such buyers members of the management company by allotting them fully paid shares therein;

(c) Undertake the management and maintenance of the development in exchange for a covenant from each member to pay an annual service charge.

A buyer's occupation rights and fully paid share in the management company would be fully transferable, but only in combination.

The same principles would apply in the case of a club. Buyers would become members in the same way, and with similar rights. In this case the property would have to be vested in trustees.

2. Planning Permission

Application for permission to develop a timeshare facility would be considered on the same basis as any other resort development. Since the accommodation would be occupied all year round, the standard would have to be similar to that required for permanent occupation.

In general, most authorities in tourist areas favour such developments since they bring the benefits of all year round occupancy as compared with conventional holiday homes, and no difficulties are anticipated on this score.

Some authorities require a restriction on the number of weeks a buyer may purchase so as to avoid the possibility of permanent use by a single owner.

3. Management and Maintenance

It is essential that there should be adequate arrangements for the cleaning and maintenance of units, and the existence of a management company is an essential prerequisite. Such a company should be empowered to carry out these duties in return for an annual management charge to cover:

- Laundry costs
- Telephone rental charges
- Cleaning costs (wages and materials)
- Periodic painting and refurbishment
- Repairs and renewals of equipment (e.g. TV sets)
- Upkeep and maintenance of grounds, access roads, etc.
- General repairs
- Insurance (fire, flood, theft, accidental damage, etc.)
- Management salaries

A certain amount ought to be set aside each year to cover major replacements (e.g. carpets, furniture, etc.).

In the longer term an owners' association may wish to take over these activities from the management company, and some thought needs to be given to making this possible.

This annual service charge is an object of some suspicion as far as many would-be buyers are concerned, and in some countries there is legislation to protect buyers against developers who set the charge low initially and then raise it excessively later. There is no such legislation in Britain, but it is not uncommon for the charge to be linked to the retail price index as a form of protection.

Owners normally pay for gas, electricity and telephone calls themselves, but arrangements have to be made to meter these services and bill the owners.

Consideration could be given to the provision of extras (e.g. maid hire or a letting service) on a supplementary charge basis.

THE SUTTON MANOR HOTEL

Sutton Manor was built during the 1820s as the residence of a retired British Indian Governor. It remained in private hands until the early 1950s, when it was bought by owner-manager James Edgar and converted into a hotel. Edgar's policy has been to keep as many of the traditional country-house features as possible, so that the public rooms have retained an 'Edwardian' character, with many of the original prints and photographs and a number of big game trophies giving a 'Raj' flavour. Modernization and upgrading have been limited to the installation of central heating and double glazing throughout.

The original frontage has been preserved intact. The building commands a good view over sloping grounds down to the edge of the lake, where there is a boat house and private mooring. Fishing rights are owned by the hotel, and guests are encouraged to make use of them.

The hotel has 20 twin or double bedrooms, 11 of which have bathrooms en suite and the others showers and washbasins. All the rooms have colour TV sets and tea-making equipment. The furnishings are in keeping with the general character of the building. The rooms are well proportioned, with the majority having good views across the grounds and lake.

The reception area, restaurant and bar are furnished and decorated to conform to the same image, conveying an image of discreet, old-fashioned comfort and luxury.

The dining room seats a maximum of 48 covers, which has tended to inhibit its use as a public restaurant during the peak season. The service is conventional silver service, and the cuisine is designed to be in keeping with the hotel's traditional 'Edwardian' character. The kitchen is equipped along old-fashioned lines, and meals reach the dining room via a dumb waiter.

Some of the original facilities have had to be discontinued due to high operating costs and relatively low demand. The turkish bath and the gymnasium are no longer used, though the fixtures and some of the fittings remain; horses are no longer kept; and the private mooring currently has no boats other than two oared dinghies used for fishing.

Some of the outbuildings are used for staff accommodation, while the remainder still serve their original functions of lodge, garages, kennels, stables, gardeners' stores, potting shed, greenhouses, etc.

The Sutton Manor Hotel employs one full-time and one part-time Receptionist, one full-time and one part-time Housekeeper, a Chef, Head Waiter, Barman and two Gardeners/Maintenance men. It relies largely upon temporary staff (e.g. students) to cope with seasonal fluctuations. Labour turnover among full-time staff is low.

Edgar ran the hotel in a friendly, paternalistic manner, arguing that the Sutton Manor's ambience and clientele required a relatively old-fashioned management approach. Like the previous management of the Dee Hall, he prided himself upon being 'a good employer' and was generous in terms of sick pay and sympathetic and understanding towards employees with family problems. Again, as in the Dee Hall the staff regarded his administration as 'firm but fair'.

In keeping with this principle, systems and procedures were deliberately kept old-fashioned, especially since it was found that many guests favoured this. The hotel still records bookings on a traditional conventional chart and continues to prepare guests' bills by hand. Equipment is conventional, though well maintained, and there has even been something of a move to re-introduce old-fashioned reconditioned items (e.g. vacuum cleaners).

The hotel does not handle group tour bookings on a regular basis. A number of small 'one-off' group bookings have been negotiated, but in general this type of demand coincides with the more profitable private or travel agency bookings. These include a considerable number of American or Dominion visitors to the Lake District.

The Lake District is situated in the northernmost peninsula of England. The M6 motorway which borders the district enables the motorist (over 80 per cent of all visitors arrive by car) to reach the region from most of the main cities comparatively quickly. A journey from London to Kendal can take less than 4.5 hours. For those who are not travelling by road, direct rail journeys are possible from most urban centres.

The Lake District has managed to retain an atmosphere of remoteness, peace and beauty. It has no less than nine conservation areas designated as being outstanding. The scenery is breathtaking, a unique combination of mountains, fells, pastures and forested valleys filled with lakes and farms. The picturesque stone-walled villages and farms blend into the natural surroundings and add to their beauty. A Cumbria Tourist Board survey showed that 59 per cent of the visitors mentioned the scenery as the main attraction of the area.

Cumbria also has fine stretches of coastline between Morecambe and the Solway. The Tourist Board lists one hundred historic houses, gardens and castles, plus fine museums and art galleries, and plans are now being considered for providing accommodation for orchestral and stage presentations.

Cumbria has strong literary associations, and many thousands of tourists come each year to visit Wordsworth's cottage and the scenes frequented by the Lakeland Poets, not to mention the originals of the Beatrix Potter stories. It is also an area rich in folklore and steeped in tradition. This is reflected in the fairs, festivals and sports events which are held throughout the year and which attract many sightseers.

The hills, lakes and coast lend themselves to a variety of outdoor pursuits such as fell walking, mountaineering, pony-trekking, fishing, sailing, canoeing and swimming.

A survey carried out throughout the season by P. A. Management Consultants Ltd found that 80 per cent of all the people interviewed came from outside the region. This underlines the fact that tourism is a major source of income for the area and its 50,000 residents. For every eight residents who saw benefits in tourism only one felt that the disadvantages outweighed the advantages.

Characteristics of British Tourists to Cumbria

Purpose of visit (%):

Holiday	77
Visiting friends	8
Business	12
Other	3

Economic status (%):

AB	30
C1	29
C2	29
DE	12

Age of tourist (%):

Under 24	23
25–44	43
Over 45	34

Time of year (%):

Jan./Feb./Mar.	10
Apr./May/Jun.	25
Jly/Aug./Sep.	48 (8% in September)
Oct./Nov./Dec.	17

SUTTON MANOR HOTEL: FINANCIAL INFORMATION

Profit and Loss Account for the Year Ended 31 March 1985

	Rooms £	Food £	Beverage £	Total £
Sales	49,000	101,600	35,000	185,600
Less Cost of goods sold		61,000	18,600	79,600
Departmental gross profits	49,000	40,600	16,400	106,000
Less Departmental expenses:				
Wages and staff costs	4,500	26,500	10,200	41,200
Laundry	2,200	1,200	400	3,800
Glass/china		500	300	800
Fuel		600		600
	6,700	28,800	10,900	46,400
Departmental profits	42,300	11,800	5,500	59,600
Less Unapportioned expenses:				
Administration				10,000
Repairs and maintenance				5,600
Depreciation				4,300
Heating and lighting				4,200
Advertising				2,700
Rates and insurance				4,300
Other expenses				3,500
				34,600
Net profit for period				£25,000

115

Balance Sheet as at 31 March 1985

	Cost £	Depreciation £	Net £
Fixed assets:			
Land and buildings	200,000	5,000	195,000
Furniture and equipment	45,000	35,000	10,000
	245,000	40,000	205,000
Current assets:			
Stocks		15,000	
Trade debtors		6,600	
Cash at bank and in hand		200	21,800
Less **Current liabilities:**			
Creditors		13,000	
Bank overdraft		2,700	15,700
Net current assets			6,100
Total assets			£211,100
Represented by:			
Capital (as at 1/4/84)		205,300	
Add Net profit		25,000	
		230,300	
Less Drawings		19,200	£211,100

Revenue Estimates for Calendar Year 1985

Estimated Accommodation Revenue

Season	Weeks	Room occupancy		Room rates per week		Estimated revenue		
		D(15) %	S(5) %	D £	S £	D £	S £	Total £
High	13	95	100	140	80	25,935	5,200	31,135
Mid	13	70	70	90	60	12,285	2,730	15,015
Low	26	30	30	50	40	5,400	1,440	6,840
						43,620	9,370	52,990

Notes: D = Doubles (total 15)

      S = Singles (total 5)

      High season is Jun./Jly/Aug. Mid season is Apr./May and Sep.

      Low season is Oct./Nov./Dec. and Jan./Feb./Mar.

Estimated Revenue from Meals Served (Residents and Chance)

	Breakfasts	Lunches	Dinners
High season	3,048	2,850	4,550
Mid season	2,230	2,000	3,500
Low season	1,512	1,500	1,800
	6,790	6,350	9,850
Rate (ASP)	£2	£3	£7
Total revenue	13,580	19,050	68,950
Total			£101,580

Estimated Bar Sales
Bar sales for the past three years have been approximately one-third of food sales, so:

£35,000

THE SUTTON MANOR: MENUS

Breakfast Menu

Bon Appetit

Continental   £2.50

Orange and Grapefruit Juice
Breakfast Rolls and Toast
Butter and Preserves
Tea   Coffee   Hot Chocolate

English   £3.00

Choice of:
Orange or Grapefruit Juice
Porridge or Cereal
Eggs – Boiled, Poached or Scrambled
         or with Bacon, Sausage or Tomatoes
or Grilled Kippers
Breakfast Rolls and Toast
Butter and Preserves
Tea   Coffee   Hot Chocolate

Table d'Hôte Menu

Available Daily – £3.50

Soup of the Day
Egg Mayonnaise
Prawn Cocktail

***

Lasagne Verdi Bolognaise
Roast Breast of Chicken and Bacon
Baked Filet de Plie Mornay
Braised Liver and Onions

***

Selection of Potatoes and
Vegetables of the Day

***

Black Forest Gateau
Bread and Butter Pudding
Semolina and Raspberry Jam
Ice Cream

***

Coffee

A la Carte Menu

Hors d'Oeuvres

Cocktail de Crevettes Marie Rose North Sea Prawns served on a bed of lettuce and covered with a creamy Marie Rose sauce	£1.75
Bisque d'Homard Fine Champagne Cream of lobster soup with brandy	£1.25
Cuisses de Grenouilles sautée Fines Herbes Frogs' legs sauteed in butter with garlic and chopped parsley	£4.50
Blanchailles Daiblées Deep fried whitebait served with lemon and cayenne pepper	£1.00
Saumon d'Ecosse Fumé Specially selected smoked Scotch salmon	£2.75

Jambon de Bayonne Thin slices of Bayonne Ham carved from our own smoke-cured joint	£2.00
Terrine de Foie de Volaille Chef's own chicken liver pâté	£1.45
Oeufs Pochés Continental Poached eggs on collops of pâté coated with a rich Madeira sauce	£0.95
Consommé Parisienne Beef consommé with a julienne of potatoes and leeks	£0.60
Hors d'Oeuvre Riche Your selection from our trolley	£1.75

Les Poissons

Sole de Douvres Grillée ou Meunière Whole Dover sole grilled or cooked in butter	£6.00
Truite de Rivière Hussarde River trout boned, filled with fish forcemeat, braised in white wine, coated with cream sauce and then glazed	£4.00
Coquille St Jacques au Noilly Scallops poached with Noilly Prat, minced mushrooms and white wine sauce	£3.75
Homards au Choix Lobster cooked to your choice	As available

Les Entrées

Suprême de Volaille Valois Breast of chicken, egg and breadcrumbed, cooked in butter, garnished with stuffed olives and béarnaise sauce	£4.00
Rognons Sautés Bouchère Sliced lambs' kidneys tossed in butter with chipolatas and squares of fillet of beef with a Madeira sauce	£3.95

Escalope de Veau Chevreuse   £4.50
Escalope of veal sauteed with a Marsala sauce and
garnished with artichoke bottoms filled with mushroom
and noisette potatoes

Tournedos Sauté Dubarry   £5.75
Prime fillet steak cooked in butter with a wine sauce and
garnished with small florets of cauliflower mornay

Selle de Lièvre St Hubert   £3.60
Jugged saddle of hare

Faisan Souvaroff   As available
Pheasant cooked in a sealed cocotte dish with diced
truffles, foie gras and cognac

Les Grillades et les Rôtis

Caneton Rôti à l'Anglaise   £9.00
Whole roast duckling with savoury seasoning and bacon

Carré d'Agneau Rôti aux Herbes de Provence   £4.20
Roast best end of lamb sprinkled with herbs from
Provence

Côte de Boeuf Rôtie Charollaise (2 persons)   £10.00
Roast rib of beef with a red wine sauce, sliced marrow
and parsley

Longe de Veau Rôtie Renaissance (2 persons)   £12.00
Loin of veal with artichoke bottoms garnished with
carrots and turnips and cauliflower coated with
hollandaise sauce

Entrecôte Maître d'Hôtel   8 oz   £3.75
Sirloin steak served with maître d'hôtel   10 oz   £4.25
butter, straw potatoes   12 oz   £4.95

T-Bone Steak   £5.50
A prime 16 oz T-bone steak accompanied by mushrooms
and fried potatoes

Rump Steak   £4.50
Grilled rump steak garnished with water cress and
allumette potatoes

Filet de Boeuf	8 oz	£4.75
Fillet steak garnished with mushrooms,	10 oz	£5.25
tomatoes and fried potatoes	12 oz	£5.75

Guéridon

Steak Diane £5.95
A thin fillet steak cooked with chopped shallots,
mushrooms, flamed in brandy and coated with Madeira
sauce

Steak au Poivre £5.95
Fillet steak coated in crushed black peppercorns,
flamed with brandy and enriched with cream

Rognons Flambés £4.50
Veal kidneys cooked in butter and served with a red
wine sauce

Steak Tartare £5.95
Finely chopped beef steak seasoned and presented with
a raw egg yolk and garnished with capers, anchovy
fillets, finely chopped onion and parsley

Légumes et Salades

Bouquetière de Légumes (2 persons) £2.00
Our selection of freshly cooked vegetables in season

Pommes et Légumes au Choix £0.50
Potatoes or vegetables cooked as you wish

Les Salades £0.75
Your choice of salads with French, lemon or Roquefort
dressing

Les Entremets et les Savouries

Crêpes Suzette (2 persons) £3.50
Thin pancakes cooked at your table with sugar and
butter, orange and lemon juice, Grand Marnier and
flamed with brandy

Soufflé Rothschild (2 persons) £3.00
A light and delicate soufflé with brandied candied
fruits

Voiture de Pâtisserie £1.00
A selection from our pastry trolley

Canapés Ferodos £0.80
Grilled mushrooms, bacon and stuffed olives on toast

Huître Florentine As available
Oysters poached with a mornay sauce and leaf spinach
and served in their shells

Les Fromages £1.00
A selection of English and continental cheeses served
from the trolley

Les Cafés

Coffee and Cream	£0.50
Gaelic Coffee	£1.30
Calypso Coffee	£1.30
Mocha Coffee	£0.65

Sutton Manor – approach from the drive.

PLANS

Plans of the Sutton Manor are provided (see pp. 124–129).

Sutton Manor – rear view from artificial lake.

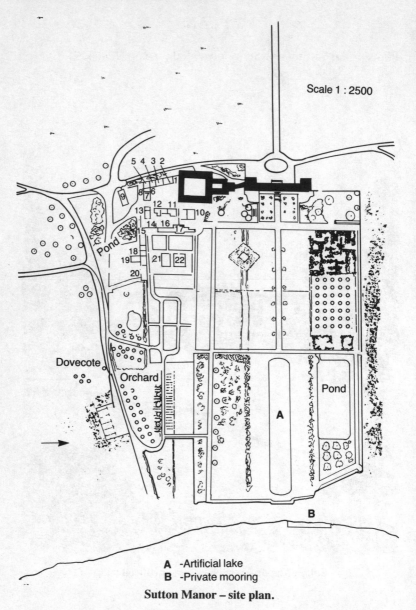

Scale 1 : 2500

A -Artificial lake
B -Private mooring

Sutton Manor – site plan.

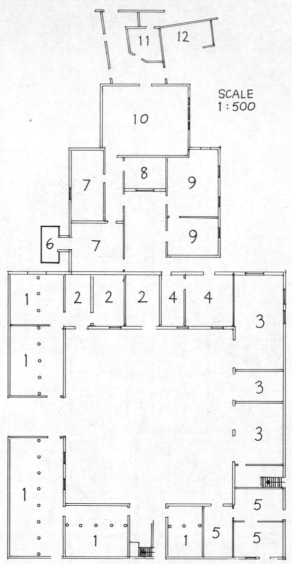

Sutton Manor – ground floor plan: kitchen and outbuildings.

SCALE
1 : 500

Key:

1. Stables
2. Saddle and tack rooms
3. Garages and coach house
4. Stores
5. Hotel manager's accommodation
6. Game store
7. Larder
8. Cold store
9. Laundry
10. Kitchen
11. Boiler
12. Wood store

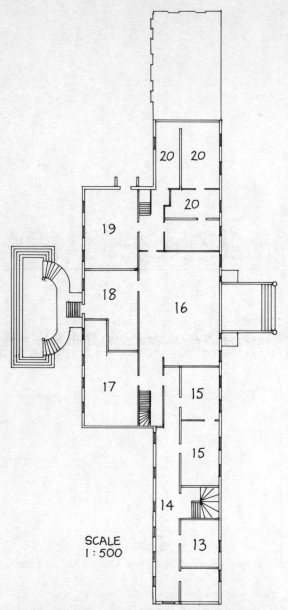

Sutton Manor – ground floor plan: main building.

Key:

13. Wine store
14. Servery/dumb waiter
15. Housekeeper's stores
16. Billiards room
17. Television lounge
18. Turkish bath
19. Gymnasium
20. Changing rooms/showers/toilets

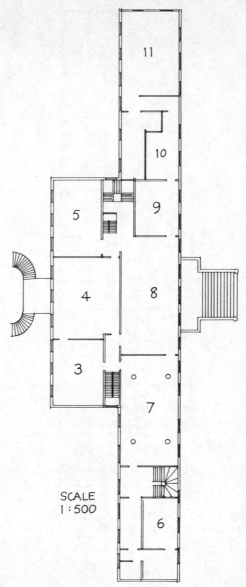

Sutton Manor – first floor plan.

Key:

3. **Reception**
4. **Hall**
5. **Residents' lounge**
6. **Manager's office**
7. **Dining-room**

8. **Cocktail lounge**
9. **Bar**
10. **Store**
11. **Library**

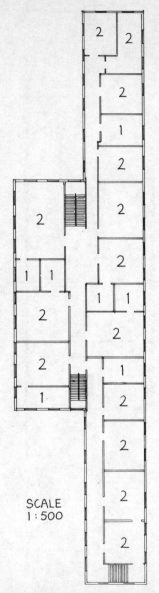

SCALE
1 : 500

Sutton Manor – second floor plan.

Key:

1. **Bathrooms**
2. **Bedrooms**

SCALE
1:500

Sutton Manor – third floor plan.

Key:
1. Bathrooms
2. Bedrooms

INSTRUCTIONS

Prepare a report for the Board of Duchy Hotels regarding the feasibility of acquiring the Sutton Manor Hotel with a view to timeshare development.

SUGGESTIONS

Your report might usefully include:

- A financial analysis of the Sutton Manor to date
- An assessment of the hotel's current value and recommendations as to offer price and means of payment
- A critical appraisal of the timeshare proposal
- A review of the current accommodation and food and beverage operations and an assessment of changes required in the light of the proposed conversion to timeshare operation
- Design proposals and plans relating to the proposed conversion to timeshare operation
- Marketing and sales promotion proposals relating to the proposed conversion to timeshare operation
- Capital financing, pricing and budget proposals
- Projected revenue and cost estimates
- A review of the legal and management implications of the proposed conversion to timeshare operations.

CHAPTER 8

THE PALATINE ALES 'PUB GRUB' CASE

The next case is even more implementation orientated than the last. There is not a lot of doubt about the desirability of what is being proposed: the problem lies in anticipating the kind of difficulties which will arise and in devising effective and imaginative solutions.

Palatine Ales is not in fact a particularly large company, but it is the largest we have used so far. This makes it a more complex organization, which in turn means that there are more interest groups to satisfy. Management's role thus becomes a kind of balancing act (this is sometimes called the 'stakeholder' theory), and it has to be even more persuasive than ever in 'selling' its proposals.

Palatine's size also raises another problem. Public companies have to publish an annual report and accounts. This can be a somewhat daunting document, but it would be unrealistic for us to simplify it too much. By choosing a relatively small company, we have at least avoided the complications of group or consolidated accounts! Incidentally, this choice also justifies the 'north-western' bias of our cases, for north-west England is at the time of writing still one of the strongholds of the small to medium regional brewery.

CASE STUDY

PALATINE ALES PLC

Palatine Ales is a family controlled north-western brewery company which has its head office at St Helens. It cannot be compared with the 'big six' national brewers (Allied, Bass, Courage, Watneys, Whitbread, and Scottish and Newcastle), and it is significantly smaller than the main 'regional' brewers (i.e. Greenall Whitley and Boddingtons), but it nevertheless retains a market niche as a regional brewery specializing in distinctive, good quality beers.

The company's products have been praised by CAMRA, and catchphrases from past advertising campaigns such as 'What's

131

Mine? A Palatine!' are still in common use within the region. Palatine now brew their own house lager ('Palatinate') and have joined up with a number of other smaller regional breweries to market independent products such as Dulverton Cider.

Palatine was formed from a group of small regional breweries in 1960 in response to the contemporary brewery 'merger boom'. Its main elements were Watson Breweries (St Helens) and Weaver Ales (Northwich), both old-established and reputable companies. The main architects of the amalgamation were Cecil Lester of Weaver Ales and John Watson of Watson Ltd. Lester (the older and more experienced of the two) became Managing Director with Watson as his deputy. They worked harmoniously together, and succeeded in preserving the company's independence during the remainder of the 'merger boom' years. In 1965 Watson became Managing Director and Lester (now at retiring age) Chairman. Thereafter Lester devoted less and less time to the business, and he finally died in 1980. Meanwhile Watson had succeeded in rationalizing the company's production and distribution system, and even managed to expand modestly through a judicious process of agreed mergers with smaller family-owned breweries.

Palatine currently operate 153 public houses in the north-west, distributed as follows:

Cheshire	64
Merseyside	27
Greater Manchester	17
Central Lancashire	25
North Lancashire	20
	153

Of these, 54 are company owned and operated by salaried managers, while the other 99 are tied houses owned and operated by tenants. Custom and practice determine whether any particular pub is managed or tenanted, and the company has no formal policy in favour of either alternative. The proportions of managed to tenanted houses has remained roughly constant for the past ten years. The company also supplies beer etc. to another 197 free houses and clubs within the region.

The rationalization process involved concentrating the production of standard draught beers at the Watson brewery at St Helens. The brewing plant there was modernized during the early 1970s and subsequent investment has kept it in line with current technology. Weaver's Northwich brewery was also retained, and the production of the new 'Palatinate' lager was concentrated there in a second redevelopment phase during the later 1970s. Other and smaller breweries coming under Palatine control were closed down and the premises sold (the proceeds helping to finance the redevelopment programmes). This process necessarily involved some redundancies, but it was found that many of the reductions could be achieved through natural wastage, and it was possible to offer a considerable number of employees transfers to the St Helens or Northwich breweries.

Both breweries are now up-to-date and efficient plants, and it can be assumed that neither will require extensive re-investment for some years yet. The St Helens brewery (traditional draught beers) is currently operating at *c*. 85 per cent capacity (75–80 per cent is generally reckoned to represent break-even point), but the Northwich brewery (mainly lager) is currently achieving no more than 65 per cent. This is a matter of some concern for the Board, but it anticipates that the situation will improve as lager consumption continues to increase.

The company used to have a small chain of off-licences, but these were sold off in 1972 to help finance the brewery modernization programme. Since this made the running of separate off-sales facilities at the public houses uneconomic, these were gradually eliminated.

Up till 1983 there were only two operating departments, namely production (which covered brewery operations and distribution) and sales (which covered public house operations as well as marketing). During 1983 sales was split into Estates (responsible for all public house operations) and Marketing, and the Marketing Manager was given a seat on the Board. Recently, Mike Lester has recognized the need to co-ordinate and develop the catering side of the operations, and has set up a small Pub Catering Department under the Estates division.

The company's present management structure is as follows:

John Watson
(Chairman/Managing Director)

Dan Jones	Mike Lester	Tom Watson	George Phillips
(Marketing)	(Estates)	(Production)	(Finance)
	Public Houses	Brewery	

133

John Watson (62) is the senior family representative and controller of the family shareholding. He has a non-vocational Oxbridge degree but has been thoroughly trained in the operations of the family business and is a shrewd and capable manager with some 32 years of practical experience (plus 5 years in the army, where he rose to the rank of major). He accepts the need to introduce more formalized management procedures in principle, but in practice continues to operate a highly personal and informal management system marked by the absence of rigid rules, working practices or job specifications. This ambiguity is reflected in his attitude towards the younger members of the Watson and Lester families. He has encouraged them to obtain relevant academic or professional qualifications, but has also insisted that they 'work their way up' through the departments in the traditional style. Observers have commented that he is less tolerant and sympathetic when dealing with them than with other colleagues or outsiders.

Mike Lester (37) is Cecil's nephew and the only surviving member of the Lester family. John Watson tends to regard himself as Mike's adopted father, but Mike has inherited the substantial Lester shareholding and this gives him a considerable amount of independence (which is not always to John Watson's taste). He has an economics degree plus postgraduate management training, but has been in the business for 12 years. He began in the then Sales Department and has retained a special interest in the public house operations side of the business.

Tom Watson (34), John's son, has a science background and is in overall charge of the main brewery operations. He is not as forceful a character as Mike Lester, with less in the way of business acumen or entrepreneurial flair, but he is technically competent, and is not only respected as a manager but liked for his loyalty towards his subordinates.

Dan Jones (64) has no formal qualifications but has had long experience in the distribution and sale of beers, wines and spirits as Marketing Manager for Palatine. He is a 'Palatine Man' through and through, and his loyalty to John Watson is unquestioned.

George Phillips (56) is non-family but has been with Palatine for 16 years. He is a cost accountant and also acts as company secretary in respect of share issues, pensions and the like. He is also very much a 'Palatine Man'.

There are two part-time non-family directors, Fred Cox (58), an accountant by training, and Les Thomas (68), the retired chairman of a smaller brewery absorbed in 1975.

In general, opposition to John Watson's ideas tends to come from Mike Lester, while Jones, Cox and Thomas generally support the Chairman. Tom Watson's interests are mainly technical, and he takes little interest in the retail side of the business.

Palatine consider themselves to be good employers, though their attitudes and practices might be thought to be slightly old-fashioned and paternalistic in that there is no measure of staff performance or formal mechanisms or procedures for staff management. John Watson dislikes trade unions, and the rest of the Board share this view. The company has not offered its staff very much by way of incentives and perquisites in the past, and salaries are considered to be average rather than generous. There is no profit-sharing scheme and no mechanism whereby employees (other than directors) can purchase shares in the company. However, working conditions are reasonable for the trade (i.e. pub tenants and managers work long hours, but no more so than those of comparable companies), job security is high, and the staff are, by and large, loyal to the firm. Labour turnover is relatively low, and the majority of staff (including both tenants and managers) have over five years' service.

There is a relatively small administrative staff, all employed at the company's St Helens head office, and a number of brewery workers who are split more or less equally between the St Helens and Northwich sites. Practically all of these work a normal five-day week. Sales and delivery staff also work five-day weeks. There is provision for overtime to cope with periods of peak demand, but with demand generally static or declining during the early 1980s the need for this has only arisen during periods of particularly hot weather (beer sales are notoriously weather sensitive). Staff are entitled to 24 working days holiday per year in addition to double time for each statutory holiday worked. As is common in the brewing industry, they are also entitled to a generous allocation of the company's products.

Managers receive rent-free accommodation and a basic salary. This is negotiated on an individual basis, but Mike Lester has been trying to relate all new contracts to turnover between a range of £5,250 (turnover £80,000) to £7,500 (turnover £200,000 plus). There is an annual profit bonus on liquor sales: this is pensionable and averaged £800 in the last financial year. Managers also receive a stock allowance to cover entertainment and staff drinks: this ranges between £25 and £40 per week according to beer sales. Managers are members of the company pension scheme, which allows for retirement at 60 and is generally recognized to be reasonably generous.

Managers are expected to keep their house open for all the hours permitted by law. Total hours are not prescribed because of the special nature of the trade (i.e. exemptions, extensions and licensing hours which vary from district to district). In common with other staff, managers are entitled to 24 working days holiday per year in addition to double time for each statutory holiday worked plus up to four days off in lieu.

Managers are required to put down a small security deposit, but all equipment is provided by the company, which also pays staff wages and overhead expenses, together with a small additional honorarium (currently 5 per cent of husband's salary) to the manager's wife for looking after the domestic accommodation. There are currently no female licensees, so the question of a 'husband's honorarium' has never been raised.

The Federation of Public House Managers (FPHM) currently represents 85 per cent of Palatine's managers. Its regional organizer has negotiated a company agreement with the Board, the main points of which are detailed above. The FPHM is concerned about possible future developments in the licensed house sector, and is anxious to protect both the short-term and long-term interests of its members. Accordingly, it has submitted a claim (dated 30 April 1985) requesting:

1. An across-the-board increase of £100 per manager

2. 28 days annual holiday

3. A clothing allowance of £500 per annum

4. 7 days off in lieu of public holidays (in addition to the agreed double time)

5. A payment (equivalent to time and a half on normal workdays and double time on Sundays and public holidays) in respect of any additional hours worked as a result of extensions to licensing hours

6. An allowance of £1,000 per annum in respect of any new technology introduced (e.g. computerized tills)

Tenants and their staff are not carried on the company payroll. Tenancy agreements are for a maximum of seven years, though they are normally renegotiated. The numbers of tenancies expiring each year are approximately equal. Retiring tenants sell their tenancy to a purchaser who must be approved by the company: applications are handled by Estates, usually by Mike Lester personally. As is customary in the trade, tenants purchase all fixtures and fittings (including bar furnishings), initially from the company and subsequently from the outgoing tenant. Goodwill is specifically excluded from the selling price (again, this is customary in the trade). The price is invariably agreed on the basis of figures submitted by an independent licensed property valuer. The price at which tenancies change hands is currently within the range £115,000 to £155,000.

Tenants are required to purchase all liquor, soft drinks and bar items such as crisps and tobacco from Palatine, though at a discount, and they are expected to make their living from the profits after deduction of rent (paid to Palatine), wages, rates, lighting and heating, etc. The company remains responsible for property insurance and maintenance.

Approximately 88 per cent of the tied pubs offer some form of lunchtime catering, including 5 per cent which have restaurants attached. Palatine have traditionally left this side of the business to the licensee's individual initiative. Some licensees have seen catering as a profitable sideline and invested their own cash and other resources into developing it, while others have either not been interested or have lacked the capital to do so, and have accordingly only provided minimum facilities.

The company reserves the right to veto or restrict the provision of additional facilities such as juke-boxes, fruit machines, pool tables, etc., but does not specify from whom these must be hired or demand a proportion of the takings (this attitude is in contrast to most of the national brewery companies and does something to explain why Palatine are regarded as good employers/landlords by their licensees).

The company has a June to May financial year. The operating divisions prepare their preliminary budgets for the following year in March. The company holds a 'budget preview' meeting in April, attended by all the Executive Directors and Senior Operational Managers. At this meeting the divisions review their performance in the current year and present and answer questions on their plans for the following year. Afterwards the company's accounting staff prepare a preliminary financial budget for finance and revenue.

Sales staff are given an opportunity to review their estimates when the current year's figures are finalized in June, and the budget is then submitted to the Board for final approval.

Control is exercised by the Board, which meets monthly. The Directors receive updated management accounts for each division. These show monthly actual, monthly forecast, cumulative figures and an updated forecast for the current year, and comparative figures for the preceding year. The Board takes necessary action on the basis of these figures.

If any operating division wishes to incur capital expenditure, it submits an appraisal form to the Finance Director. Major capital expenditures are always considered by the Board.

The company's Directors' Report and Statement of Accounts for the year ended 31 May 1985 are provided below.

PALATINE ALES PLC: DIRECTORS' REPORT AND STATEMENT OF ACCOUNTS 1985

Chairman's Statement

I am pleased to report pre-tax profits up from £5,531,000 to £5,999,000. Earnings per share increased from 17.8p to 18.0p. These trading results enable your Directors to declare a final ordinary dividend of 5.55 pence per share as opposed to 5.10 pence last year, an increase of 28.3 per cent.

Our philosophy remains one of offering our customers a good quality product at reasonable prices. This has served us well in the past and continues to do so now. Our traditional 'Palatine Bitter' and 'Weaver' brands have held their own in a market which is generally static, even in areas of high unemployment. Our 'Palatinate Lager' brand has continued to enjoy steady growth, supported by a series of TV advertisements.

During the year 5 additional premises were added to our estate, and 3 older houses unsuitable for further development were disposed of. We have pursued a vigorous programme of refurbishment of our tied and tenanted estate. These changes will strengthen your company's competitive position, which continues to be centred exclusively within Cheshire, Greater Manchester, Lancashire and Merseyside.

We have maintained our share of the free trade market, despite intense competition and considerable pressure on margins. Again, sales of 'Palatinate Lager' have made encouraging progress.

Capital expenditure has been directed mainly at improving packaging and distribution. We are now producing our traditional 'Palatine Bitter' in large cans and 2-litre PET bottles suitable for the take-home trade, and our sales force has made encouraging progress in placing these on off-licence and supermarket shelves. This is still a relatively small aspect of our operations as yet, but the sector is one of the major growth areas and we cannot afford to neglect it.

We owe a particular vote of thanks to our loyal and hard working employees for all their efforts during the year. We are very conscious of the fact that we remain a North Western company supported by North Western customers and a North Western staff.

With our long tradition of effective management and careful attention to quality we have a bright future as an independent company.

John Watson
Chairman   30 June 1985

Report of the Directors
The principal activities of the Company were the brewing, wholesaling and retailing of beers, wines and spirits, minerals and the ownership and management of public houses.

A review of the Company's business for the year ended 31 May 1985 is provided within the Chairman's Report and the accompanying financial statements.

The following Directors served throughout the year. Mr F. Cox, Mr D. Jones, Mr M. Lester, Mr G. Phillips, Mr L. Thomas, Mr J. Watson (Chairman), Mr T. Watson. The Director who retires by rotation is Mr F. Cox who, being eligible, offers himself for re-election.

No Director has or had during the period any material interest in any contract of significance to the Company's business.

The Company is not party to any arrangement to enable any Director or his family to acquire benefit through the acquisition of any shares, debentures or loan stock of any other company.

Interests of the Directors and their families as at 31 May 1985 were as follows:

| | Ordinary shares of 25p each | |
	31/5/84	*1/6/85*
Beneficial interest:		
F. Cox	745,200	1,390,500
D. Jones	194,400	165,600
M. Lester	1,350,000	1,350,000
G. Phillips	799,200	936,000
L. Thomas	535,500	882,000
J. Watson	1,840,500	1,800,000
T. Watson	270,000	270,000
Trustee interest:		
J. Watson	450,000	450,000

Details of substantial holdings of the share capital of the Company at 31 May 1985 are as follows:

- North Western Insurance plc: 1,350,000 ordinary shares at 25p each (7.5 per cent of the issued share capital)

The close company provisions of Section 282 Income and Corporation Taxes Act do not apply to the Company.

During the year the following sums were contributed:

- For charitable purposes: £5,682 (1984 £7,274)

- For political purposes to the Conservative Party: £2,000 (1984 £2,000)

Messrs Fiddle and Perks have indicated their willingness to continue in office as auditors and a resolution to re-appoint them will be proposed at the forthcoming annual general meeting.

By Order of the Board etc.

John Watson
Chairman   30 June 1985

Profit and Loss Account for the Year Ended 31 May 1985

	Note	1985 £000s	1984 £000s
Turnover	3	33,838	30,805
Operating charges	4	28,121	25,547
Trading profit		5,717	5,258
Income from fixed asset investments	6	732	683
		6,449	5,941
Finance charges	7	450	410
Profit before taxation		5,999	5,531
Taxation	8	2,334	2,281
Profit after taxation		3,665	3,250
Dividends paid and proposed	9	1,000	920
Retained profit for the year		£2,665	£2,330
Earnings per ordinary share (pence)	10	20.33	17.80

Balance Sheet as at 31 May 1985

	Note	1985 (£000s)	1984 (£000s)
Fixed assets:			
Tangible assets	11	26,340	23,500
Investments	12	6,100	5,690
Current assets:			
Stocks	13	1,806	1,400
Debtors	14	4,400	4,600
Cash at bank and in hand		1,600	1,800
		7,806	7,800
Creditors: amounts falling due within one year	15	4,600	5,100
Net current assets		3,206	2,700
Total assets *less* current liabilities		35,646	31,890
Creditors: amounts falling due after more than one year	16	2,590	1,500
		£33,056	£30,390

	Note	1985 (£000s)	1984 (£000s)
Capital and reserves:			
Called-up share capital	17	4,500	4,500
Share premium reserve	18	3,750	3,750
Revaluation reserve	18	16,265	16,265
Profit and loss account	19	8,541	5,875
		£33,056	£30,390

J. Watson

G. Phillips   Directors, 15 June 1985

Sources and Applications of Funds Statement for Year Ended 31 May 1985

	1985 (£000s)	1984 (£000s)
Source of funds:		
Profit before taxation	5,999	5,531
Depreciation	859	773
Profit on sale of investments	—	(134)
Total generated from operations	6,858	6,170
Funds from other sources:		
Proceeds from sale of investments	4,213	2,340
Loans issued	1,090	—
Repayment of loans by customers	—	2,460
	12,161	10,970
Application of funds:		
Dividends paid	927	787
Taxation paid	2,702	2,580
Purchase of fixed assets	3,699	1,245
Purchase of investments	4,623	3,670
Debentures redeemed	—	1,408
Increase/decrease in working capital	£210	£1,280

	1985 (£000s)	1984 (£000s)
Movement in working capital		
Stocks	406	610
Debtors	(200)	340
Creditors	204	755
Net liquid funds	(200)	(425)
Funds from other sources	£210	£1,280

Notes to the Accounts

1. Accounting Principles
(a) The accounts have been prepared under the historical cost convention. The Company's accounting policies are consistent with previous years. Goodwill, which arises where the cost of acquiring subsidiary companies exceeds the net assets taken over, is written off directly to reserves. Net assets are incorporated at their fair values.

(b) The charge for taxation is based on the profit for the period and takes into account taxation deferred or accelerated because of timing differences between the treatment of certain items for accounting and taxation purposes. Provision is made for deferred taxation only to the extent that it is probable that the tax will become payable, and is at the rate at which it is estimated that the tax will be paid.

(c) No depreciation has been provided for in respect of freehold and long leasehold licensed properties. It is the Company's policy to maintain properties comprising its licensed estate in such condition that their value to the business of the estate as a whole is not affected by the passage of time. As a consequence, any provision for depreciation would, in the opinion of the directors, be immaterial, and no such provision has been made.

Other assets, with the exception of motor vehicles, are depreciated on a straight line basis from the beginning of the year following purchase. Motor vehicles are depreciated on a straight line basis beginning in the year of purchase. The periods over which assets are depreciated are as follows:

Brewery and office buildings	50 years
Brewery plant	25 years
Other plant and equipment	5–10 years
Casks	10 years
Fixtures and fittings (licensed properties)	10 years
Motor vehicles	5 years

(d) Repairs to properties and fittings in licensed properties are written off as incurred.

(e) The stock valuation basis is as follows:

- *Raw materials:* at the lower of cost and net realizable value.

- *Beer in process:* at production cost, including raw materials, duties where applicable, direct labour and expenses plus the appropriate proportion of overhead expenses.

- *Stocks purchased for resale and stocks at managed houses:* at the lower of cost and net realizable value.

- *Stocks in bond:* at the cost of placing into bond.

- *Other stocks* (e.g. cases, packing materials and other consumables): at the lower of cost and net realizable value.

(f) The Company funds pension liabilities by payments to insurance companies and a managed fund. These funds are invested and managed independently of the finances of the Company. Contributions in respect of current service and the cost of augmenting existing pensions are charged against profits.

2. Comparative Figures
The comparative figures for 1984 are included.

3. Turnover
Turnover comprises sales, rents, and other trading income by the Company but excludes value added tax. The analysis of turnover by activity and geographical market has not been disclosed because the Company has only one major activity, which is carried out solely within North West England.

144

4. *Operating Charges*

	1985 £000s	1984 £000s
Raw materials	7,811	6,080
Customs duty paid	7,030	5,460
Changes in stocks etc.	406	370
Staff costs	5,858	4,565
Auditors' remuneration	23	18
Depreciation	859	669
Repairs to property	976	770
Other charges	5,158	7,615
Totals	£28,121	£25,547

5. *Staff Costs*

	1985 £000s	1984 £000s
Wages and salaries	5,191	4,035
Social security costs	445	355
Pension costs	222	175
Totals	£5,858	£4,565

The average number of employees in each week during the period was:

Administration	65
Production	144
Sales, distribution and managed houses, including 534 part-timers	673
Total	882

Staff costs include emoluments in respect of Directors as follows:

	£
Fees	15,000
Executive remuneration	76,000
Executive pension contributions	33,000
Total	£124,000

145

	£
Emoluments (excluding pension contributions) of the Chairman who is also the highest paid Director	36,000
Other directors:	Number
£5,001–£10,000	2
£10,001–£15,000	—
£15,001–£20,000	2
£20,001–£25,000	2

6. Income From Fixed Asset Investments

	1985 £000s	1984 £000s
Listed investments	424	365
Other investments	308	318
Totals	£732	£683

7. Finance Charges

	1985 £000s	1984 £000s
Bank interest	154	204
Interest on debentures	266	135
Other interest	30	71
Totals	£450	£410

8. Taxation

	1985 £000s	1984 £000s
Corporation tax on profit for year	2,550	2,351
Deferred taxation	(216)	(70)
Totals	£2,334	£2,281

146

9. Dividends

	1985	1984	1985	1984
	Pence per share		£000s	
Ordinary shares:				
Interim dividend paid	1.95	1.90	352	343
Proposed final dividend	3.60	3.20	648	577
Totals	5.55	5.10	£1,000	£920

10. Earnings per Ordinary Shares

The calculation of earnings per share is based on earnings of £3,665,000. The weighted average of shares in issue during 1985 was 18,027,432.

11. Tangible Assets

	Brewery £000s	Licensed premises £000s	Plant £000s	Total £000s
Cost or valuation 31/5/84	6,000	14,500	3,000	23,500
Net additions during year		2,200	1,499	3,699
Depreciation			(859)	(859)
Net Book Values	£6,000	£16,700	£3,640	£26,340

12. Investments

	Listed	Trade	Total
At 1 June 1984	1,140	4,550	5,690
Additions	250	2,840	3,090
Disposals/repayments	(190)	(2,490)	(2,680)
At 31 May 1985	1,200	4,900	6,100

The market value of listed investments at 31 May 1985 was £2,950 (1984 £2,690).

13. *Stocks*

	1985 £000s	1984 £000s
Raw materials	455	406
Beer in process	297	255
Stocks purchased for resale	320	288
Stocks at managed houses	308	266
Stocks in bond	78	72
Other stocks	142	113
Total stocks at replacement cost	£1,600	£1,400

14. *Debtors*

	1985 £000s	1984 £000s
Trade debtors	2,964	3,154
Other debtors	867	875
Prepayments	569	571
Totals	£4,400	£4,600

15. *Creditors: Amounts Falling Due Within One Year*

	1985 £000s	1984 £000s
Trade creditors	1,418	1,590
Bank loans and overdrafts		
Bills payable	4	5
Corporation tax	1,876	2,244
Other taxes and social security	654	685
Proposed dividends	648	576
Totals	£4,600	£5,100

16. Creditors: Amounts Falling Due After One Year

	1985 £000s	1984 £000s
9% Unsecured loan stock 1991/1995	1,500	1,500
12% Unsecured loan stock 1996/2000	1,090	
Totals	£2,590	£1,500

(a) The 9% unsecured loan stock is redeemable at par on 31 May 1995 or, at the Company's option, in whole or in part at any time in the preceding five years.

(b) The 12% unsecured loan stock is redeemable at par on 31 May 2000 or, at the Company's option, in whole or in part at any time in the preceding five years. £10,000 was purchased on the open market and cancelled during the year.

17. Share Capital

	1985 No. 000s	1985 £000s	1984 No. 000s	1984 £000s
Ordinary shares of 25p each:				
Authorized	25,000	6,250	25,000	6,250
Allotted, called-up and fully paid	18,000	4,500	18,000	4,500

18. Share Premium and Revaluation Reserves
There were no changes in these accounts during the year.

19. Profit and Loss Account

	£000s
Balance at 31 May 1984	5,875
Retained profit for the year	2,665
Balance at 31 May 1985	£8,540

Five Year Record of the Company
(£000s unless stated otherwise.)

	1985	1984	1983	1982	1981
Turnover	£33,838	£30,805	£28,157	£25,867	£23,976
Profit before taxation	5,999	5,531	4,338	4,014	3,639
Taxation	2,334	2,281	1,688	1,562	1,416
Profit after taxation	3,665	3,250	2,650	2,452	2,223
Extraordinary items *less* taxation	0	0	556	234	0
Profit after taxation and extraordinary items	£3,665	£3,250	£3,206	£2,686	£2,223
Earnings per ordinary share (pence)	20.3	17.8	14.9	12.4	11.4
Dividends per ordinary share (pence)	5.55	5.10	4.85	4.65	4.25

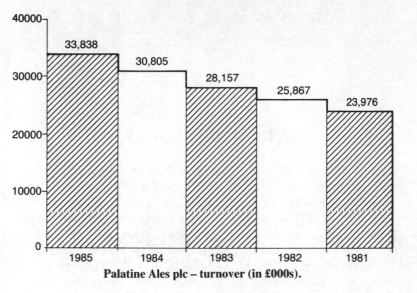

Palatine Ales plc – turnover (in £000s).

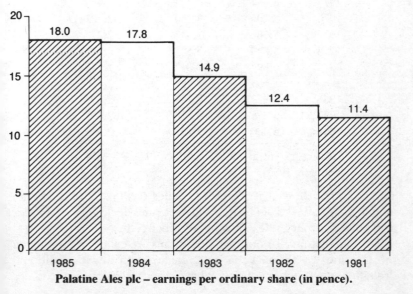

Palatine Ales plc – earnings per ordinary share (in pence).

To: Board of Directors

From: Mike Lester

Date: 31 March 1985

Subject: Public House Catering

SECTION 1: INTRODUCTION

I am concerned about the disappointing performance of the public houses. Figures show that beer sales by volume have actually shown a decrease. At first sight this would appear to be a new development, but in reality it reflects a long-term trend which has been masked until now by a series of new acquisitions which have increased total sales each year.

This trend is not restricted to our own company. National figures show a marked shift away from consumption of alcohol in pubs and clubs and towards consumption at home, as demonstrated in the following table:

Consumer spending (1980 prices: £ millions)

	Beer	On-licence	Off-licence
1974	5,396	7,508	1,882
1975	5,584	7,383	1,959
1976	5,705	7,250	2,223
1977	5,684	7,342	2,273
1978	5,840	7,583	2,533
1979	5,897	7,817	2,740
1980	5,655	7,455	2,686
1981	5,352	7,132	2,697
1982	5,285	6,870	2,707
1983	5,400	7,135	2,915

(Sources: Central Statistical Office 1974–82: MMD Estimate 1983)

These figures show that while beer sales declined overall by an annual figure of −0.5 per cent, on-licence sales declined by −1.1 per cent and off-licence sales grew by +5.5 per cent.

The implications for our own operations are clear, and are made more serious by the fact that our real strength lies in traditional draught beers. Such increases as have occurred in on-licence sales have tended to be in products such as lager, cider, wines and spirits, many of which we purchase from outside suppliers in the form of proprietary brands.

Although average sales per outlet have shown a slight decrease in each of the last five years, some of our licensees have done much better than others. Analysing the figures, we have discovered that those outlets which offer cooked food have actually increased their sales of all beverages, including liquor, whereas those which either do not sell food or provide only snacks such as crisps and sandwiches have shown significant decreases in liquor sales.

Again, this is in line with national trends, as the following table indicates:

Trends in consumer expenditure on food catering

	1977 %	1979 %	1981 %	1983* %
Restaurants	33	27	25	25
Take-aways	32	33	34	34
Pubs	17	22	24	25
Hotels	18	18	17	16

* Estimated.   (Source: *Euro-Monitor*)

It must be remembered that the *total* expenditure has increased each year.

It is clear that food sales in pubs are increasing faster than those in any other sector of the catering industry. Some of our major competitors actually forecast that they will exceed bar sales by the early 1990s. They can not only compensate for declining liquor sales, but can even arrest and reverse that trend.

Competitors such as Bernis, Whitbreads, Bass Charrington, Greenall Whitley and Boddingtons have all begun to offer carefully thought out catering packages which are popular because they meet customer expectations in terms of food quality, quantity, atmosphere, service and price.

Palatine, on the other hand, remains loyal to the image of the pub as basically a 'boozer', and few of our establishments really encourage patronage by women and mixed company.

We suggest that if our company wishes to stop the decline in its drink sales and arrest the erosion of its market by competitors developing their units into catering outlets, it ought to enter the catering market as quickly as possible.

SECTION 2: PROGRESS TO DATE

During 1984, prior to the establishment of the Pub Catering Department, we initiated two pilot schemes. Both have now been running for over 12 months, and the operating figures indicate that in addition to encouraging returns from food sales, drink sales have increased by approximately 10 per cent. Details of the two schemes and outline operating figures are provided below.

Scheme 'A': The Lord Derby
We co-operated with the manager of the Lord Derby, a large pub at Churchtown, Southport, and financed the addition of a restaurant, which commenced operations on 1 January 1985. The cost of the restaurant and ancillary improvements was £150,000.

The Lord Derby: Weekly Sales, Costs and Profits Analysis

	1984		1985	
	£	£	£	£
Sales:				
Lunches	1,700		2,250	
Dinners	—		4,000	
Bar	3,700	5,400	5,500	11,750
Less Food/beverage costs		2,430		5,287
Gross profit		2,970		6,463
Wages, salaries		1,404		2,820
Net margin		1,566		3,643
Operating expenses:				
Rent/rates	270		470	
Heat/light	162		294	
Depreciation	135		470	
Promotion	135		294	
Cleaning etc.	135		235	
Miscellaneous	54	891	117	1,880
Net profit before tax and payment of manager's salary		£675		£1,763

We estimate that approximately 24 of our pubs meet the criteria for development along these lines, namely:

1. Adequate space for the development of restaurant facilities (e.g. room for both restaurant, kitchen with separate entrance, toilet facilities and staff areas).

2. Adequate car parking space.

3. Access to an appropriate market.

The average cost of these conversions would be approximately that of the Lord Derby.

Scheme 'B': The Navigation
We also co-operated with the managers of three of our smaller town centre pubs (the Moorcroft at Oldham, the Navigation at Northwich and the Volunteer at Warrington) in setting up 'Pub Grub' operations. The starting dates varied, but results for the year ended 31 March 1985 are shown below.

Average Food Sales Per Unit For Year Ended 31 March 1985

	£	£
85 covers per day @ £2.70 each		77,560
Less Food cost		31,020
Gross profit		46,540
Less Staff/wage costs		15,510
Net margin		31,030
Less Operating expenses:		
Rent, rates	600	
Heating, lighting	1,000	
Depreciation	3,000	
Promotion	1,000	
Cleaning	600	
Miscellaneous	500	6,700
Profit on food sales		£24,330

Drink sales averaged £180,000 per unit, showing an increase of approximately 10 per cent over the period.

We estimate that approximately 30 of our units could be developed in this way. The limitations preventing the addition of full restaurants in these units are generally a combination of the following:

1. Lack of space for development due to town centre locations, building restrictions, etc.

2. Lack of car parking space (again mainly due to town centre locations).

3. Inappropriate markets (e.g. due to proximity of large numbers of restaurants, perception by customers of them as 'boozers' or 'drinking men's pubs' or customer preference for fast food).

Space for the addition of kitchens is generally limited in these houses. It has been suggested that we could derive considerable economies from the use of prefabricated kitchen units which could be 'added on' at the side or rear. At least one of our regional competitors is planning to use such units.

We have not yet examined the implications of the structural or cost implications of this proposal in detail, but it is hoped to have preliminary drawings and outline cost estimates available prior to any Board Meeting called to discuss this issue. Our surveys indicate that such units would have to be restricted to dimensions appropriate to the Navigation.

We feel that any such development would necessarily be linked to the introduction of standardized menus. A proposal to this effect follows in Section 3.

SECTION 3: 'PUB GRUB' MENU PROPOSAL

The menu pioneered in the three Scheme 'B' pilot outlets is one based around an assortment of pies, backed up by a limited selection of other traditional pub food. The reasons for this choice were as follows:

1. Nationally, there has been a marked increase in the sale and consumption of pies. In addition, there have been increases in the sale and production of more upmarket pies.

2. The pie is native to both Cheshire and Lancashire. It is estimated that three-quarters of the region's population eat pies regularly both at home and outside.

3. Simplicity of preparation. Most pies taste best after they have been cooked, allowed to cool and then reheated.

4. Simplicity of service. Pies are suited to limited food service facilities. They retain heat well and do not spoil rapidly.

5. The possibility of a high gross profit margin.

6. Suitability in terms of 'image'. Palatine are a regional brewery with a strong Cheshire–Lancashire identity, and we felt that a pie-based menu was particularly appropriate.

The menu used has offered a choice of half a dozen regular pies and a daily 'special'. Price for the main courses included vegetables or salad from a self-service salad bar. Smaller 'children's' pies were available for £1.00. Small selections of starters and sweets were also made available. A typical menu was:

Starters:	£
Melon	0.75
Homemade Soup	0.75
Main courses:	
Steak and Kidney Pie	2.00
Cheshire Pork and Apple Pie	2.00
Chicken and Leek Pie	2.00
Fylde Turkey and Chestnut Pie	2.00
Haddock and Prawn Pie	2.00
Vegetarian Pie	2.00
'Speciality' Pie	2.00
Cold Meat Platter	2.50
Scampi	3.50
Sirloin Steak	4.50
Sweets:	
Ice Cream	0.60
Apple Pie	0.95

The Vegetarian Pie was changed every month or so. The 'Speciality' Pie might be rabbit, game or some more exotic variant.

The pies were produced within the public houses themselves by the manager's wife or catering assistant on the basis of recipes prepared by this department. Materials were purchased locally. Given the circumstances, some variation in quality was inevitable, but this was more pronounced initially than towards the end of the pilot period.

The pies were found to have a shelf life of approximately one week. Appropriate maximum and minimum stock-holding levels were established for each unit. Whoever was responsible for the

157

catering would 'top up' pie stocks as part of their normal afternoon duties. The figures below indicate the average daily demand pattern, though there were both local and seasonal variations:

Item:	Max.	Min.
Steak and Kidney	36	24
Pork and Apple	24	16
Chicken and Leek	24	16
Turkey and Chestnut	24	16
Haddock and Prawn	12	8
Vegetarian	12	6

Menu costings were established following a process of discussion with the pub's caterer. Average costings were as follows:

Cheshire Pork and Apple Pie (makes 6)

	£
2 lb loin pork	2.05
4 rashers bacon	0.30
8 oz onion	0.05
12 oz pippins	0.20
2 oz brown sugar	0.10
2 oz butter	0.15
Quarter pint light ale	0.25
6 pastry tops	1.05

£4.15   ÷ 6 = 68p per portion

Chicken and Leek Pie (makes 6)

	£
3.5 lb chicken	2.52
8 oz onion	0.05
2 sticks celery	0.05
4 oz tongue	0.40
6 leeks	0.25
2 tbs parsley	0.20
6 pastry tops	1.05

£4.52   ÷ 6 = 75p per portion

Rabbit Pie (makes 6)

	£
1 large rabbit (2–3 lb)	1.50
4 oz butter	0.25
8 oz onion	0.05
6 oz streaky bacon	0.20
1 lemon	0.30
4 sprigs thyme	0.30
0.75 pint beef stock	0.05
6 pastry tops	1.05
4 oz breadcrumbs	0.05
2 oz suet	0.05
1 tbs parsley	0.05
1 egg	0.10
	£3.95

£3.95 ÷ 6 = 65p per portion

SECTION 4: UNIT PLANS

We attach plans in respect of the Lord Derby, Southport (see pp. 160–162), and the Navigation, Northwich (see pp. 163–166). These are included in order to illustrate the kind of structural and situational constraint we face in developing 'Pub Grub' operations. Our public houses vary in terms of individual design and construction, but the plans provided are typical of the two types of unit distinguished in the Preliminary Report, and it may be assumed that appropriate proposals will be suitable for other units falling within the same category.

It should be noted that these represent *current* plans (i.e. after conversion). In the Navigation's case the ground floor food preparation area was obtained by converting an old-fashioned and unwanted small private bar: similar areas suitable for conversion cannot be guaranteed in more than 50 per cent of the units, though equivalent areas could be made available in the remainder through 'building out'.

———

A week or two before the Board Meeting at which the Pub Catering proposals are due to be considered, John Watson calls you in for a talk.

'I think Mike's proposal is going to run into some opposition', he

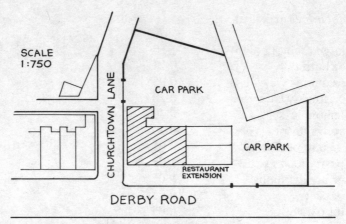

The Lord Derby – location plan.

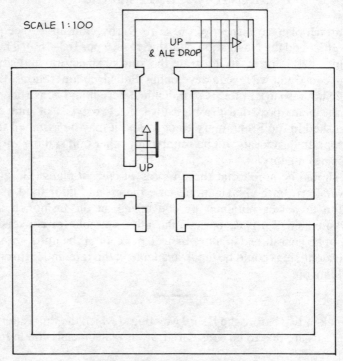

The Lord Derby – basement plan.

160

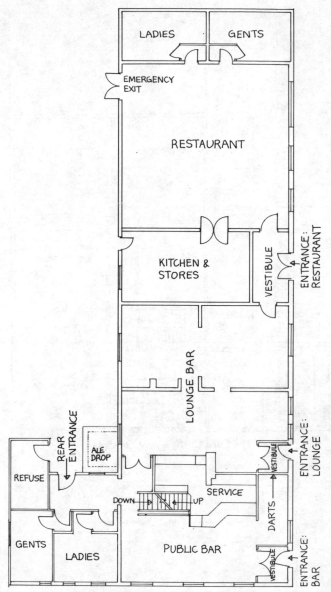

The Lord Derby – ground floor plan.

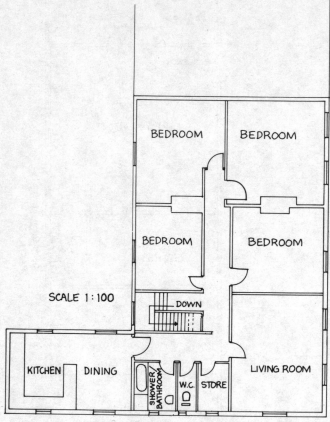

SCALE 1:100

The Lord Derby – first floor plan.

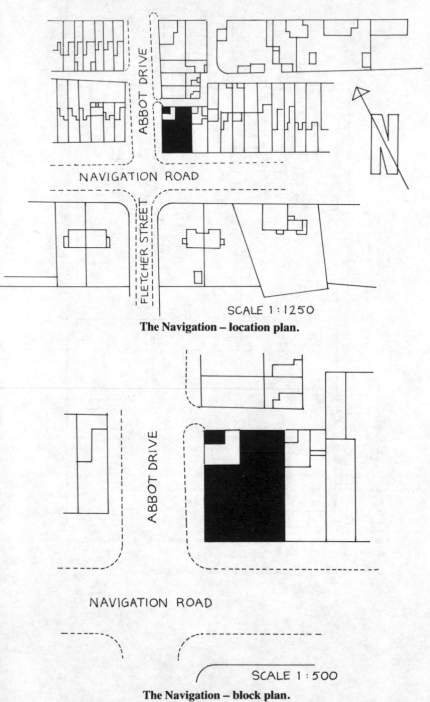

The Navigation – location plan.

The Navigation – block plan.

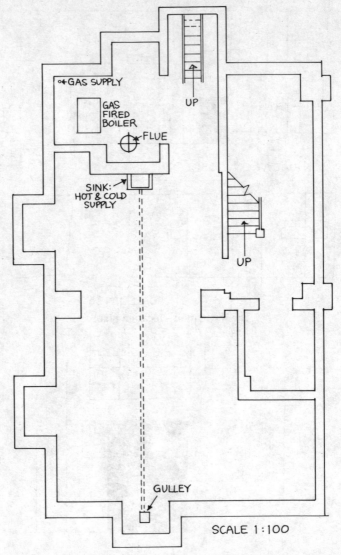

The Navigation – cellar plan.

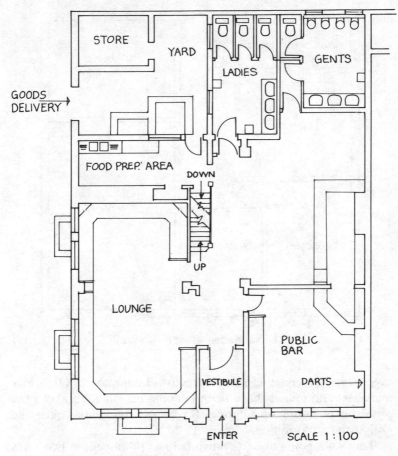

The Navigation – ground floor plan.

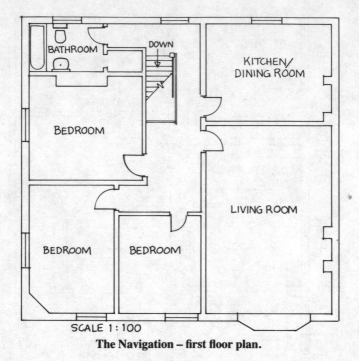

The Navigation – first floor plan.

says. 'Dan Jones is being a bit obstructive. I think some of the older managers and tenants have been bending his ear a bit about the problems of setting up catering. He keeps talking about keeping faith with our "traditional" market!

'Tom's not going to be as much help as I'd hoped, either. He's saying that we ought to be moving a bit up market and selling wines, spirits and cocktails to the 18–25 age group. He wants us to develop our own line of ready-bottled cocktails: I can see he's got his eye on a new bottling plant! He says pub grub would conflict with this approach and that all we need is a good line in savouries.

'All in all, it looks like being a tough battle. Maybe they're right. Can you let me have a report setting out your views on where we should go from here?'

INSTRUCTIONS

Prepare a report for John Watson as Managing Director of Palatine Ales, evaluating Mike Lester's 'Pub Grub' proposal and submitting your conclusions and recommendations.

SUGGESTIONS

Your answer might usefully include:

- An analysis of Palatine's Annual Report and Accounts

- An assessment of the possible outcomes of the negotiations with the pub managers' representatives, together with your recommendations regarding negotiating strategy

- A critical assessment of the 'Pub Grub' proposal in the context of the general economic situation described

- An analysis of the operating statements supplied by the two representative pubs

- An analysis of the proposed menu in terms of costs and quality, with recommendations regarding modification or extension if appropriate

- A review of the structural and re-equipment implications of implementing the 'Pub Grub' proposal, including outline plans and a suggested layout for a prefabricated kitchen unit

- Capital financing and budgeting proposals relating to the above

- A marketing and promotional plan relating to the above

- A review of the legal and personnel implications of the proposed introduction of 'Pub Grub'.

CHAPTER 9

PALATINE ALES PLC: THE TAKEOVER ATTEMPT CASE

So far, we have looked at the external environment in only a very general kind of way. We have simplified the competitive situation to a considerable extent, and by choosing largely family-owned businesses have managed to avoid questions of ownership. This has allowed us to concentrate on the problems of running an established business.

In reality, public companies not only compete against other: they also have to guard against the ever-present risk of takeovers. This raises all kinds of additional problems which we can't afford to ignore, even though it forces us to consider a new and higher level set of issues.

We have chosen to look at these through the medium of Palatine Ales, the company we introduced you to in the previous case. You will remember that Palatine were a brewery company considering expansion into the field of 'Pub Grub'. We trust that you came up with some workable proposals. Unfortunately, before you are able to implement any, an emergency arises and you have to shelve them, at least for the time being (this is a fairly typical feature of management life).

The emergency consists of a takeover bid by a larger and more aggressive company. The story can be told through selected and edited documents. You will have to read through these to discover whether the attempt is ultimately successful or not. As we said when introducing an earlier case, managers have to learn to make sense of all kinds of technical documents, so we are not going to apologise for making you wade through a selection of press releases, offers and the like. These are realistic enough, for we have copied layouts and borrowed phrases from genuine examples, but we must stress that no resemblance is intended to any actual organization or individual.

Some knowledge of developments in the brewing industry during the 1960s, 1970s and early 1980s is also necessary in order to understand the background, and the case accordingly includes a summary of these. Note, however, that they do not take account of post-1985 changes.

CASE STUDY

INTRODUCTION

Before any action could be taken with respect to Mike Lester's 'Pub Grub' proposals, the calm at Palatine was broken by a sudden takeover offer by Anglo-Welsh Breweries plc. Anglo-Welsh was a relatively new consortium of previously independent regional breweries put together during the later 1970s by a shrewd and aggressive operator named K. Midas, who made no secret of his ambition to build it up until it rivalled the major national breweries. Palatine were an attractive target since the new group was still relatively weak in the North West.

The Palatine Board were united in their rejection of the Anglo-Welsh bid. However, there was a significant number of private and institutional shareholders. If enough of those accepted the Anglo-Welsh offer, control might well pass to the conglomerate, with embarrassing and even financially damaging consequences for the existing Board members. They decided to fight.

During the ensuing months, a fierce battle was raged. It was conducted by various means, including letters and even tapes sent to shareholders, press releases, national advertisements and a good deal of 'lobbying' of financial correspondents and commentators.

Palatine's general structure and current financial situation remain as detailed in the preceding case.

PART I: THE CONTEXT

The brewing industry currently consists of over 80 firms which between them own over 140 breweries. It is estimated to employ some 750,000 persons in all, with 57,700 persons in direct manufacturing and a further 30,000 in public houses. It contributes nearly 7 per cent of all state taxes in the form of VAT and excise duty.

Post-war trends in beer, spirits and wine consumption can be seen from the following table:

Year	Beer (m. barrels)	Spirits (m. gallons)	Wine
1945	31.0	8.3	4.4
1950	25.8	9.8	11.6
1955	23.6	11.5	16.9
1960	26.6	14.2	27.0
1965	29.9	19.1	36.4
1970	33.5	18.0	48.4
1975	38.5	20.7	77.5
1980	40.0	21.2	116.5

(Source: Economist Intelligence Unit)

Beer consumption in the early 1980s has shown a decline. The figure for 1982 was 37.8 m. barrels and for 1984 38.2 (source: MMC based on HM Customs and Excise plus Brewers' Society).

Current consumption patterns for beer can be seen from the following tables:

Beer consumption by age and socio-economic groups, 1982 (% of total)

	All beer	Lager only
18–24	23	33
25–30	27	31
35–49	25	24
50 plus	25	12
	100	100
ABs	12	10
C1s	21	21
C2s	40	42
DEs	27	27
	100	100

Average weekly beer consumption (male drinkers), 1982 (pints)

	18–24	25–35	35–49	50+
All beer	14.4	12.5	11.5	8.8
All draught	12.4	10.7	11.0	8.9
All packaged	3.9	4.2	3.5	3.2
Bitter	10.6	9.4	10.1	8.7

	18–24	25–35	35–49	50+
Draught lager	10.1	8.1	8.3	5.8
Mild	9.2	7.1	8.3	8.0
Draught Guinness	4.4	5.1	7.9	6.1
Light, pale, export	2.8	3.1	3.0	2.5
Packaged lager	3.4	3.6	2.9	2.5
	AB	C1	C2	DE
All beer	8.9	9.7	12.8	12.5
All draught	8.5	9.0	11.7	11.8
All packaged	2.8	3.2	4.1	4.0
Bitter	7.8	8.5	10.5	10.6
Draught lager	5.7	6.6	9.3	10.3
Mild	6.2	5.5	9.1	9.1
Draught Guinness	5.1	4.7	6.8	6.9
Light, pale, export	2.1	2.7	3.2	3.0
Packaged lager	2.5	2.6	3.6	3.5

(Sources: PAS Beer Market Survey)

The history of the industry is one of steady concentration. Even in the eighteenth century excise returns reveal that 12 big London breweries accounted for 25 per cent of the national production. However, there were still nearly 1,500 independent brewers operating around 6,500 separate breweries in 1900. By 1937 the number of brewery firms had been reduced to 1,000, and this process continued in the immediate post-war years. It was due to:

1. A steady decline in beer drinking per head (which forced the larger breweries to expand in order to maintain production at viable levels).

2. The development of motor transport (which expanded the economic distribution areas).

Even in 1950, however, beer production was largely regional, if not local, and there were still some 310 firms with 540 separate breweries. Relatively more of the smaller independent breweries were to be found in the North. 'National' brewers accounted for only 18 per cent of all beer production, and their brands were nearly all bottled ales, since these were more easily transported and had a longer life than cask-conditioned draught beer.

171

This situation changed radically as a result of the 'merger boom' of the period 1957–69, which saw the national brewers' share of net output rise from 18 per cent to 64 per cent. By 1970 there were only 96 companies with 177 breweries. This 'merger boom' (which became particularly frenetic between 1959–61) was due to the following factors:

1. Beer consumption fell as compared to the pre-war period, and did not pick up again to 1945 levels until 1968. As a consequence of this trend, defensive mergers took place to protect local oligopolies. A further consequence was that brewery share prices were generally depressed during the 1950s.

2. The growing realization that the industry's major asset, its licensed premises, were generally undervalued and under-utilized. Investment analysts who reviewed brewery balance sheets during the 1950s tended to add 80–100% to the book value of the assets, which usually raised their value to considerably in excess of the current market price. The merger 'scramble' of 1959–61 was largely sparked off by a bid by well-known takeover specialist Charles Clore for Watney Mann. This was defeated, partly because speculation forced the Watney shares up to a more realistic (i.e. less attractive to Clore) level, but Watney immediately launched its own series of defensive mergers, nearly doubling its size between 1959 and 1965 and giving itself national status.

3. The trend towards bottled beers (partly because bottling plant was expensive, and partly because the 'nationals' were already strong in this field) and the subsequent expansion of keg beer (which allowed draught beers to be distributed more widely).

Despite some well-publicized takeover battles, most of the mergers were 'agreed', and were indeed often initiated by the company eventually taken over. The possibility of a bid from an unwelcome quarter (notably the Canadian Carling magnate E. P. Taylor and his United Breweries, later merged with Charrington and subsequently part of Bass) was often enough to persuade the directors to approach a more acceptable company for protection. Negotiations were carried on in secret and the results were presented to shareholders as a *fait accompli*. Traditional friendships and rivalries played at least as important a part in this process as purely financial considerations.

This helps to explain the success of Whitbread's 'umbrella'

approach. In contrast to the other emerging national brewers, Whitbread initially did not attempt to take over smaller firms, but rather to take minority shareholdings (15–30 per cent) and conclude arrangements whereby the local firm bottled and sold Whitbread's brands. This policy preserved the independence of the smaller breweries. It had to be modified in 1961 when it became clear that a minority holding did not provide a certain defence against a determined takeover, but Whitbread continued to retain minority holdings in a number of regional brewers, which enabled them to retain their independence.

By 1968 some 73 per cent of beer production was in the hands of seven major national firms, while there had been further progress towards the consolidation of a number of medium-sized regional breweries, largely at the expense of the smaller local firms. The major national breweries themselves began to either acquire or be acquired by non-brewing companies so as to form larger conglomerates such as Allied-Lyons (formed when Allied Breweries took over the catering group J. Lyons in 1978), Grand Metropolitan (formed when Grand Met Hotels took over Truman Hanbury and Buxton in 1971 and Watney Mann in 1972) and Imperial (formed when Imperial Tobacco acquired Courage Breweries in 1972). The major groups at this period were:

Group	Tied outlets	Market share
Bass	8,150	c. 20%
Allied-Lyons	c. 7,500	14–16%
Whitbread	7,850	13–14%
Grand Met. (Watney etc.)	c. 6,500	12–13%
Scottish & Newcastle	1,500	11%
Imperial (Courage)	c. 4,000	8%

(Source: Economist Intelligence Unit)

The trend towards consolidation slowed down somewhat in the 1970s. There were still 82 companies with 147 breweries in 1975, and 81 with 142 breweries in 1980. The beginning of this slowing down process is frequently said to be Allied's failure to take over Boddingtons in 1969 (Boddingtons were part of the Whitbread 'umbrella', and Whitbread threw its weight behind the family shareholders). There were certain factors which contributed to the survival of the smaller breweries during this period, namely:

1. There was a general upturn in beer consumption, which

allowed production to approach optimum rates (generally reckoned to be 75–80 per cent of capacity), thus offering higher returns on capital.

2. A dramatic rise in fuel costs after 1973, which affected the national brewers' distribution costs more than the smaller regional ones'.

3. The Campaign for Real Ale (CAMRA), which led to an unexpected but genuine revival of interest in distinctive local brews.

However, it has been suggested that long-term factors still favour further consolidation. These include:

1. Uncertainty over long-term beer consumption patterns (there was a fall in total beer consumption in the early 1980s).

2. The probability of technological developments which will reduce unit costs.

3. The growing importance of lager, which offers similar advantages to the nationals as bottled beer and keg beers in the past (i.e. a standardized product offering considerable manufacturing economies of scale and well suited to national advertising and distribution).

4. The probability that only the larger organizations will have the financial resources to ride out recessionary periods.

5. The fact that many of the smaller companies are still family controlled or influenced (these ownership patterns reduce their access to financial resources and thus their ability to ride out recessions).

The current (1980s) rankings of the major brewers vary somewhat from product to product:

Estimated market shares 1982 (% volume sales)

Brewer	On-sales		Off-licence
	Ales	Lager	
Bass	17.5	25.0	9.0
Allied-Lyons	14.0	13.5	11.5
Whitbread	11.0	12.0	12.5
Grand Met. (Watney etc.)	10.5	13.5	10.0

Brewer	On-sales Ales	Lager	Off-licence
Imperial (Courage)	9.0	9.0	7.0
Scottish & Newcastle	13.0	12.0	12.5
Others	25.0	15.0	37.5
	100.0	100.0	100.0
Total m. barrels	24.9	12.3	5.1

(Sources: Economist Intelligence Unit and trade estimates)

The 'big six' are as follows:

- *Bass* (main draught brands Bass itself, Worthington, Stones, Blackpool and Highgate) is traditionally strong in the light, pale and export ales sectors, has important lager brands (Carling and Hemeling) and is also well represented in the fast growing packaged bitter market (through its canned Stone's bitter). The group also has leisure interests (Coral and Pontins) which provide 25 per cent of its turnover.

- *Allied* (draught brands include Ansells, Benskins, Double Diamond, Ind Coope, Taylor Walker and Tetley) are particularly strong in the light, pale and export ales market (its strongest brand is Long Life, which was the first canned beer on the market and is currently leader in the export segment, but it also produces Skol and Arctic Lite). In 1978 the group diversified into catering and beverages through the acquisition of J. Lyons.

- *Whitbread* (draught brands include Chesters, Flowers, Fremlins, Mackesons, Strongs, Trophy, Whitbread and Wethereds) are strong in the so called 'real ales' sector. It was the first UK brewer to set up a home sales division and was for years undisputed leader in this field. Its best known lager (Heineken) is second only in the take-home sector to Guinness, and it has 41 per cent of the take-home brown ale market. It retains interests in other regional breweries, and has expanded into steak houses (Beefeater).

- Grand Metropolitan's *Watney* (draught brands include Manns, Norwich, Truman, Watney, Websters, Wilsons and Ushers) is strong in the premium lager market, with three major brands (Fosters, Holstein and a substantial share of Carlsberg) and dominates the brown ale market. It also has interests in spirits

(J & B Scotch and Gordon's Gin), together with fast food (Schooner Inns).

- Imperial's *Courage* group (draught brands include Courage itself, Simonds and John Smiths) ranks third in the light, export and pale ale market. It has a significant interest in the Harp lager consortium, and about 11 per cent of the take-home brown ale market. Like other groups it has diversified into fast food (Happy Eater) and hotels.

- *Scottish & Newcastle* (McEwans and Youngers beers, Newcastle Brown) have a relatively low holding of tied public houses (which are mainly in Scotland and the North East), but still account for a significant proportion of total beer sales, partly through sales to free houses and partly through the strong position of their brands in the off-licence trade. S & N also operate Thistle Hotels.

In addition to the 'big six', mention must be made of certain more specialized national companies, namely:

- *Guinness.* This company has no tied outlets but is completely dominant in its own market segment. Guinness is sold through all the major brewer's outlets, and accounts for 4.5 per cent of total beer sales.

- *Harp.* This company is owned by a consortium in which Guinness has by far the largest share (70 per cent). Harp, Courage and Scottish & Newcastle are the main brewers and distributors but the product (like Guinness) is sold through all the national brewers. It accounts for some 8.5 per cent of all take-home lager sales and is also sold in draught.

- *United.* This is a subsidiary of the Danish United Breweries (Carlsberg and Tuborg). These brands are brewed and distributed separately, though Carlsberg is also brewed and distributed by Watneys. Altogether, United's brands account for about 4.5 per cent of all beer and 15 per cent of lager sales.

Notwithstanding the above, there were still 67 small independent non-specialist brewery companies in 1977, together producing around 16 per cent of total beer production. Of those, 47 companies were family controlled, and family influence remained considerable in a further 17 (source: *British Drink Profile*, Halliday Associates, 1979).

The special feature of the industry in the United Kingdom is its unique set of interconnections with the retailing network through the existence of the 'tied house'. These may be either 'managed' (i.e. owned by the brewery company) or 'tenanted' (independently owned but contracted to sell the brewer's products exclusively).

The importance of the public house with respect to beer sales can be seen from the following table:

Licence	Scope	% of total
Full on	Pubs	44
Restricted on	Restaurants	
	Night clubs	13
	Hotels	
Club	Members' clubs	19
Off	Off-licences	
	Supermarkets	24
		100

(Source: Home Office)

Pubs and hotels together account for around 60 per cent of all sales. Most of the major off-licence chains are also owned by the brewers, though most of the expansion in this sector has been the result of the supermarkets' willingness to compete with the established off-licences.

The number of full on-licences fell between 1945 and 1975, though it increased again after that date:

Number of on-licences (000s) in the UK

	1945	1955	1965	1975	1980
Full	81.4	79.7	75.4	73.7	75.8
Restricted		6.3	15.8	22.0
Club	16.4	22.3	25.3	30.5	33.1
Total	97.8	102.0	107.0	120.0	130.9

(Source: Home Office)

177

The proportion of tied houses decreased in the later 1970s:

Breakdown of full on-licences (000s)

	1976	1977	1978	1979
Managed houses	14.8	14.4	14.1	14.0
Tenanted houses	36.4	36.3	36.0	35.4
Free houses	23.1	23.8	25.1	26.3
Total	74.3	74.5	75.2	75.7

(Source: Brewers Society)

This was due largely to rationalization programmes which attempted to dispose of the smaller and unprofitable public houses, though these were offset by a continuing commitment to improving the appearance and amenities of the larger remaining houses.

The 'big six' control approximately half of the UK's public houses, as is shown by the following table:

National brewers' control of licensed outlets, 1981

Brewer	On-licences	Off-licences
Bass	8,150	975
Allied-Lyons	7,600	930
Whitbread	7,100	650
Grand Met. (Watney etc.)	8,050	550
Imperial (Courage)	5,300	400
Scottish & Newcastle	1,500	225
Totals	37,700	3,730

(Source: Brewers Society)

It should be noted that the 1970s saw a trend on the part of the 'nationals' to decentralize their operations by forming autonomous regional organizations and promoting regional brands.

1978 also saw a national 'pub swap' arrangement, which was in fact forced on the national brewing companies by government pressure. The aim was to ensure that no one brewer controlled more than 40 per cent of the on-licences and 33 per cent of the off-licences in any area. The scheme was administered by the Brewers' Society and involved the exchange of some 1,000 pubs over a five year period (source: *British Drink Profile*, Halliday Associates, 1979).

The significance of the regional beer market can be gauged from the following tables:

Average weekly household expenditure on beer by region, 1981

	£pw	As % of drink expenditure	As % of total expenditure
North	4.88	75.4	4.4
Yorks & Humberside	4.43	72.3	4.3
North West	3.88	62.7	3.4
East Midlands	3.02	61.8	2.7
West Midlands	3.63	64.5	3.1
East Anglia	2.28	50.4	2.0
Greater London	2.94	45.4	2.2
South East	2.79	47.4	2.1
South West	2.46	51.4	2.2
Wales	3.48	66.0	3.2
Scotland	2.68	44.1	2.4
Northern Ireland	1.65	56.9	2.7
UK	3.25	56.9	2.7

(Source: Family Expenditure Survey 1981)

Incidence of beer drinking by region, 1982: % of respondents drinking beer in last seven days

	Men	Women	All adults
North	75	25	49
Yorks & Humberside	72	29	50
North West	74	32	52
Midlands (E & W)	70	26	47
East Anglia	65	21	42
Greater London	64	19	40
South East	62	19	40
South West/Wales	70	21	44
Scotland	69	13	40
Mainland UK	69	23	45

(Source: PAS Beer Market Survey 1982)

A regional breakdown of group strengths is difficult to obtain, partly because the industry regards these figures as confidential, partly because the brewers' north western region (i.e. Cumbria and

Lancashire, including Manchester and Merseyside but excluding most of Cheshire) does not coincide with the DTI's standard north west region (i.e. Cheshire, Lancashire, Manchester and Merseyside, but not Cumbria).

Having said this, unofficial but informed trade estimates indicate that the distribution of tied on-licensed houses in the north western region does not differ significantly from the national proportions. Since the North West had some 8,700 pubs in 1981, of which approximately 57 per cent were tied, the approximate division can be assumed to have been as follows:

Brewers' control of north western licensed outlets, 1981

Brewer	On-licences
Bass	1,080
Allied-Lyons	990
Whitbread	930
Grand Met. (Watney etc.)	1,050
Imperial (Courage)	690
Scottish & Newcastle	100
Greenall Whitley	800
Matthew Brown	500
Boddingtons/Higsons*	350
Others	2,210
Total	8,700

* Separate companies at this date but
subsequently merged
(Source: Informal trade estimates)

PART II: THE TAKEOVER DOCUMENTS

Wheeler Dealers Ltd
(Merchant Bankers)
1 Fixit Row
City of London

Press Release   **5 July 1985**

The Board of Anglo-Welsh Breweries plc ('AW') announces that it intends to make an offer ('the Offer') to acquire Palatine Ales plc

('Palatine') on the terms and conditions set out below. The Offer is in AW ordinary shares. On the basis set out below, the Offer values Palatine at £54,150,000, and each Palatine ordinary share at £3.00. Palatine shareholders are being offered a significant increase in capital value and income, plus a substantial premium over net asset value. The Offer represents an exit price earnings multiple of 14.75 times. AW has acquired, through market purchases, 18.5 per cent of the issued ordinary share capital of Palatine.

The Offer
AW will offer to acquire the ordinary shares of Palatine on the following basis:

For every 5 existing ordinary shares of 25p each in Palatine	4 new ordinary shares of £3.75 each in AW credited as fully paid

and so on in proportion for any other number of ordinary shares in Palatine.

AW already owns 3,339,250 ordinary shares in Palatine. Full acceptance of the Offer by Palatine shareholders would involve the issue of 11.8 million new AW ordinary shares (representing 32 per cent of the issued ordinary share capital of AW as enlarged by the issue) with a value of £134.1 million based on the closing middle market price of an AW ordinary share of £3.75 taken from the Stock Exchange Daily Official List for 4 July 1985 (the last dealing day before the announcement of the Offer).

The ordinary shares of Palatine which are the subject of the Offer will be acquired free from all liens, charges and encumbrances and together with all rights now or hereafter attaching thereto, including the right to all dividends and distributions (if any) declared, made or paid hereafter.

The new AW ordinary shares to be issued to Palatine shareholders will rank *pari passu* with the existing AW ordinary shares and will rank for the AW final dividend to be recommended in respect of the year ending 31 December 1985, to be paid early in 1986.

A Dividend Forecast
The Directors of AW announce that, in the absence of unforeseen circumstances, they intend to announce a final dividend of not less than 6.5p per share in respect of the financial year ending 31

December 1985. Together with the interim dividends already paid this makes a total dividend for the year of 9.75p, an increase of 15 per cent over the previous year.

Reasons for the Offer

The acquisition of Palatine will achieve a strategic extension of AW's brewing interests, and in AW's view will create a merged entity which is stronger than the sum of the two parts. In particular, it will help to realize the following objectives:

- To lay the foundations in North West England for a regional business of sufficient scale, depth of resources and range of products to compete effectively against larger operators.

- To add 153 public houses to AW's tied estate, a sector in which AW is currently under-represented in the North West, where it currently has only 187 public houses.

- To add to AW's existing range of products a number of high quality and complementary brands of beer with the capacity not only for regional development but also rapid national development through AW's marketing network.

- To merge AW's existing North West England operations into those of Palatine and to build that company on the basis of its own regional tradition, supported by continuing local beer production.

The merging of Palatine with AW will not only provide the enlarged group with additional valuable brewing facilities and tied estate, but will also provide Palatine with an immediate opportunity to compete effectively beyond its traditional boundaries while maintaining the identity of its brands, its products and its tied estate. Without such a merger, Palatine will find it difficult to grow and will ultimately decline.

Financial Implications of Acceptance of the Offer

The Offer per Palatine ordinary share is equivalent to £3.00 on the basis of the closing middle market price of an AW ordinary share of £3.75 on 4 July 1985 (the last dealing day before the announcement of the Offer).

The Offer represents an exit price earnings multiple of 14.75 times on the basis of Palatine's earnings per share of 20.3p for the year ended 31 December 1984.

The Offer represents a capital uplift for Palatine shareholders of 55 per cent over the closing middle market price of a Palatine ordinary share of 193p on 8 May 1985, the dealing day before AW commenced buying Palatine shares on the market, and an uplift of 17 per cent based on the closing middle market price of a Palatine ordinary share of 256p on 4 July 1985, the dealing day before the announcement of the Offer.

Announcement of the Offer will result in more than doubled dividend income for Palatine shareholders.

The Offer value is at a premium of 70.5 per cent to the net asset value per ordinary share of 176p derived from the Palatine published audited accounts as at 31 May 1985.

Business of Palatine
Palatine's principal activity is the brewing, bottling and sale of beers and the ownership and management of public houses within Cheshire, Greater Manchester, Lancashire and Merseyside. Palatine's brand names include 'Palatine Bitter', 'Weaver Ales' and 'Palatinate Lager'. Palatine also has a minority interest in Dulverton Cider.

Business of Anglo-Welsh
AW is one of the ten largest brewing groups in the United Kingdom. It operates its own licensed outlets through its managed and tenanted estate, principally in Wales, the Midlands, South East and South West England. The AW group operates highly efficient breweries in Birmingham, Bristol, Cardiff, London, Plymouth and Wrexham. It is a major supplier of beers and lagers to the free trade, and is also extensively involved in sales of its canned products to the home consumer through the retail grocery trade. AW's brands are household names. AW has significant interests in wines and spirits, and is also an important hotel operator.

In the year ended 31 December 1984 the profit before taxation of the AW group was £15.4m on turnover of £102.5m and earnings per share were 25.2p. In the six months to 31 July 1985 the unaudited profit of the group is expected to be £9.2m, an increase of 21 per cent over the corresponding period in the previous year.

Further Terms and Conditions
Further terms and conditions of the Offer are set out in the Appendix*.

* *Note:* A technical document not included here.

Offer Document

The formal Offer and listing particulars relating to the issue of new AW ordinary shares in connection with the Offer will be posted to the shareholders of Palatine by Wheeler Dealers Ltd as soon as practicable.

Press enquiries:
Anglo-Welsh Breweries plc   K. Midas (Chief Executive)
Wheeler Dealers Ltd   A. Smoothie

Purchase and Szell Ltd
(Merchant Bankers)
Carvup House
City of London

Press Release   **8 July 1985**

The Board of Palatine Ales plc has seen the announcement by Anglo-Welsh Breweries plc of its offer to acquire the company. The Board of Palatine Ales plc, which is being advised by Purchase and Szell, regard the offer as both unwelcome and wholly unacceptable. It is the Board's conviction that the continued independence of Palatine is in the best interests of its shareholders, employees and customers.

Shareholders are advised to take no action with regard to their shareholdings. The Board will write to shareholders when the offer document from Anglo-Welsh has been despatched.

PALATINE ALES PLC

Directors: Registered Office:
J. Watson, M. Lester, T. Watson,   The Brewery
G. Phillips, D. Jones, F. Cox, L. Thomas   St Helens
                                             15 July 1985

Dear Shareholder

As promised, I am writing to you to explain why your Board and its financial advisors Purchase and Szell consider the Anglo-Welsh takeover bid to be wholly unacceptable and why we strongly recommend you to reject it. We do not need Anglo-Welsh in order to realize our exciting potential.

Palatine's tied house trade and free trade (free houses, clubs, etc.) are well balanced. Our trade mix is regarded as right and is one reason for our consistently satisfactory trading margins.

We are acknowledged to be a well-managed and progressive company. Your Board is supported by an able and dedicated team of executives who are totally committed to Palatine and its objectives. These in turn are supported by an excellent and loyal staff.

The future for your Company as an independent is bright. Our 'Palatinate' lager is recognized as one of the best draught lagers in Britain and recently won one of the premier prizes at the European Brewing and Bottling Exhibition. Our 'Palatine Bitter' and 'Weaver Ale' brands are recognized as high quality beers, and Dulverton Cider has been making significant inroads in the take-home trade.

Does all this sound like a company which, as Anglo-Welsh claim, 'will find it difficult to grow and will ultimately decline'?

As expected, in trying to persuade you to take their shares, Anglo-Welsh have made great play of their recent growth in profits. However, these have been due to large-scale rationalization, including a reduction of nearly a quarter of their work force between 1980 and 1984. Such measures only produce 'one-off' improvements, and do not amount to real growth.

Anglo-Welsh remains significantly smaller than the major national brewers with whom it hopes to compete. Even if it were to acquire Palatine, its North Western tied house stock would only increase to some 330. In order to become a significant power within the region, Anglo-Welsh will have to acquire considerably more regional brewers, at a time when we ourselves have found such expansion increasingly difficult.

The acquisition of Palatine would result in a dilution of Anglo-Welsh's earnings per share. Further brewery acquisitions would result in even more dilution. A programme of acquisitions which results in repeated dilution would seriously undermine Anglo-Welsh's ability to diversify, whichever direction they eventually wished to go.

It is the firm conviction of your Board that you should not become shareholders in a company with such an unsound strategy.

Anglo-Welsh have stated that one of their principal objectives is 'to lay the foundations in North West England for a regional business of sufficient scale, depth of resources and range of products to compete effectively against larger operators'. But Palatine is already competing effectively against much larger operators, including Anglo-Welsh itself ! Your Company has all the necessary skills, is soundly financed, and has no need of Anglo-Welsh's 'resources' to achieve its strategic aims.

Anglo-Welsh also make the extraordinary claim that they can build our regional identity. In fact, that regional identity is already firmly established. It is this enviable strength that they are trying to acquire. If we were to be swallowed up, the credibility of our beers as genuine regional products would be destroyed. The history of the industry is littered with the names of once famous regional breweries and brands which disappeared after merging with a national company. And prices would almost certainly rise: at the moment we charge 2p to 3p less than national brewers, including Anglo-Welsh! And there would certainly be no commercial benefits if Anglo-Welsh were to substitute their own products for those of Palatine. We are firmly convinced that regional loyalty to Palatine Ales is such that if our beers were replaced by Anglo-Welsh products there would be a significant overall reduction in sales.

Anglo-Welsh also mention the 'growing pressure' on regional brewers, particularly from the ever-increasing demand for lager at the expense of ales. This may be true for some, but they are bidding for Palatine! And Palatine brew the highly successful 'Palatinate Lager'! The national market for ales is indeed flat, but 'Palatinate's' growth has more than offset that problem for us.

Anglo-Welsh's huge breweries in Birmingham, Bristol, Cardiff, London, Plymouth and Wrexham are believed to have more than enough spare capacity to brew all of Palatine's production requirements. The future of our Northwich and St Helens breweries would inevitably be at risk. Anglo-Welsh have been conspicuously silent about their intentions with regard to the continued employment of our workforce.

Moreover, many of our tied houses are relatively small pubs, many of them serving villages and rural communities. We succeed in operating them profitably, but the big national breweries regard such pubs as non-viable and tend to close them or sell them off, with inevitable consequences in the form of unemployment.

Why you should reject Anglo-Welsh's bid:

- Palatine is going from strength to strength as an independent.

- Anglo-Welsh can do nothing for Palatine.

- It seriously undervalues your Company, its record, its strengths and its prospects.

Anglo-Welsh is attempting to deprive you of the opportunity to benefit from our excellent prospects. You are being asked to give up your shares in a premium company in return for an uncertain future. Your Board and its advisors, Purchase and Szell Ltd, urge you to reject the bid. Your Directors certainly have no intention of accepting the offer in respect of their own shareholdings.

Yours sincerely

(Signed) John Watson

TAKEOVER NERVES IN THE BREWING INDUSTRY
Article in *The Financial Times*, 15 August 1985

The Government's decision not to refer Anglo-Welsh's bid for Palatine to the Monopolies and Mergers Commission has set alarm bells ringing throughout the brewing industry. Regional brewers fear that the decision may make them vulnerable to predators. Mr Nathan Trelawney of the Plymouth-based Anchor Ales said, 'If this bid succeeds there is no reason why other national brewers should not make bids for other regionally based companies.'

He warned that a decline in beer sales had left the industry with spare capacity. National groups could only find outlets for their own beer by acquiring smaller companies and shutting down their brewing plant.

Though the industry has the capacity to brew about 52m bulk barrels of beer a year the consumer is only drinking about 38m. Profits are increasingly being generated by treating pubs not just as places to sell large volumes of beer but as broader retail outlets promoting food and a range of drinks.

By and large it is the large brewers, which include Allied, Bass and Whitbread, who are leading the way in refurbishment and catering, and ownership of these retail outlets is at a premium.

But the share price of some regional brewers does not fully reflect these assets. The shares of one small Midlands brewer, for instance, reflect a valuation of less than £100,000 a pub, although they are actually commanding more than £150,000 on the open market.

Regional brewers are nervous about the Government's decision. One declined to comment on his own company's feelings, saying 'We have to be very careful. The next few months are going to be very important to us.'

Scottish and Newcastle has already launched its own bid for

Matthew Brown, the Blackburn-based brewer. Other companies seen as potentially vulnerable include Vaux (Sunderland), Greene King (Suffolk) and Dudley (Wolverhampton). Possible predators include Courage, Watney Mann and Truman. Like Anglo-Welsh, the big companies could argue that they are not heavily represented in the affected areas and therefore not creating a monopoly.

The make-up of the industry, with its six big brewers commanding about 75 per cent of total beer sales, was established in the 1960s in a wave of mergers. This left about 70 smaller regional brewers, although several have turnovers of more than £50m and one, Greenall Whitley, has sales of more than £250m a year.

Over the past 10 years the growth of the Campaign for Real Ale has reflected the rejection by a section of the public of the mass-sale brands which the big brewers were selling in apparently uniformly decorated pubs. At the same time the regionals headed a return to cask-conditioned ales. These brands included those from Boddington (Manchester) and Greene King.

These developments led to a belief that the Monopolies and Mergers Commission would be hostile to further attempts by the big six to buy more breweries. Only last year organizations such as CAMRA helped to get S & N's bid for J. Cameron (Hartlepool) referred to the Commission on the grounds that if S & N acquired Cameron's pubs it would have a monopoly of outlets in the North East. S & N dropped the bid.

However, many regional brewers are now coming under increasing competitive pressure. A reflection of this is the way they are all trying to develop their lager interests in a market where lager is growing at nearly 10 per cent per annum and is likely to command over 40 per cent of all sales this year.

Other factors unfavourable to the regional brewers include:

- Growth in the take-home trade – some 15 per cent of all beer sales – in which only a few of the larger independent brewers have national distribution.

- Competition from the national brewers in the highly competitive free trade.

- High unemployment in areas of traditional heavy consumption.

- The growing 'added value' areas such as catering in which the regional brewers have less experience.

- Diversification into other associated activities such as hotels.

The regionals, whose strength tends to be in ales, have found it hard to fight for their own-brand lagers in an image-conscious market, when the big brewers can put massive advertising spending behind their products.

While ales tend to have strong regional support, the lager market is more national. Carling Black Label (Bass), Carlsberg (Carlsberg), Heineken (Whitbread) and Skol (Allied) together share an estimated 54 per cent of the lager market. Some regional breweries such as Palatine have found good niches for their products, but many others are content to sell lagers brewed by national companies such as Whitbread, thus accepting lower margins than if they brewed their own.

The regionals argue that their presence is in the consumers' interests. They point to areas such as Manchester, the West Midlands and Nottingham where beer prices are around 61p–65p per pint as opposed to 75p–80p elsewhere. The major characteristic of these areas with lower prices, they claim, is the presence of healthy and independent brewery companies, and they conclude that such competition is of benefit to the consumer.

Whether a further wave of takeovers in the brewing industry would benefit consumers is open to debate. As one City figure said, 'As a stockbroker I am fully in support of market forces prevailing. As a consumer I am more ambivalent. After all, people go into pubs for their individuality and not because they want a clone of McDonalds.'

———

Wheeler Dealers Ltd
(Merchant Bankers)
1 Fixit Row
City of London

Press Release   **6 September 1985**

The Board of Anglo-Welsh announces that it has to date purchased 722,000 ordinary shares in Palatine at 285p per share. Anglo-Welsh now holds 4.1m ordinary shares in Palatine, representing 22.5 per cent of Palatine's issued ordinary share capital. As a consequence, Anglo-Welsh's offer for Palatine is now being increased by the addition of 25p in cash per Palatine ordinary share.

The new terms are now:

For every 5 ordinary shares   4 ordinary shares in Anglo-
                                  Welsh plus 25p in cash

All other terms and conditions remain as in Wheeler Dealer Ltd's announcement of 5 July 1985. Wheeler Dealer Ltd will post the Offer Document on behalf of Anglo-Welsh as soon as practicable.

PALATINE ALES PLC

Directors: Registered Office:
J. Watson, M. Lester, T. Watson,   The Brewery
G. Phillips, D. Jones, F. Cox, L. Thomas   St Helens
                                                 12 September 1985

Dear Shareholder

On 15 July 1985 I wrote to you in connection with Anglo-Welsh Breweries' offer for your Company equivalent to 300p per share, which the Board rejected as wholly unacceptable.

Since then, Anglo-Welsh have been able to acquire far fewer shares than they sought, with only a handful of shareholders selling. They have now formally revised their offer to the equivalent of 325p. Your Board and its financial advisors Purchase and Szell Ltd consider this revised offer to be totally inadequate and continue to recommend most strongly that you take no action in respect of your shareholding. I will be writing to you again, once Anglo-Welsh have sent out their formal offer document, to set out the reasons why you should reject the offer.

I should like to take this opportunity to thank the vast majority of our shareholders who have clearly recognized Palatine's potential and have remained unimpressed by the attempted takeover. We much appreciate your support in our fight to maintain the independence of Palatine, which your Board is convinced is in the best interests of its shareholders, employees and customers alike.

(Signed) John Watson

Wheeler Dealers Ltd
(Merchant Bankers)
1 Fixit Row
City of London

Press Release   **7 November 1985**

The Board of Anglo-Welsh announces a revised offer to acquire

Palatine on the terms and subject to the conditions set out below. Anglo-Welsh already owns 5.4m Palatine ordinary shares (representing 29.75 per cent of the issued ordinary share capital).

Anglo-Welsh will make an offer to acquire all the Palatine ordinary shares other than the ordinary shares owned by Anglo-Welsh on the following basis:

For every 1 Palatine ordinary share 1 new Anglo-Welsh share

Full acceptance of the Offer would involve the issue of approximately 14m new Anglo-Welsh ordinary shares, representing approximately 37 per cent of the enlarged issue share capital of Anglo-Welsh.

As an alternative, Palatine shareholders will be offered the opportunity to elect for cash in respect of all or part of their holding in Palatine ordinary shares. The Cash Alternative will be on the following basis:

For each Palatine ordinary share 325p in cash

The maximum cash payment by Anglo-Welsh under the Cash Alternative would be approximately £45.5m.

The Offer is final. It will not be increased and will close 21 days from the date of posting the offer document unless it has become or declared unconditional as to acceptances. Anglo-Welsh reserve the right, however, to increase the Offer or extend the closing date in the event that a competitive situation arises.

PALATINE ALES PLC

Directors:	Registered Office:
J. Watson, M. Lester, T. Watson,	The Brewery
G. Phillips, D. Jones, F. Cox, L. Thomas	St Helens
	11 November 1985

Dear Shareholder

Anglo-Welsh plc have now made a further offer for your Company which the Board continues to find unacceptable.

You may have seen the advertisements placed by Anglo-Welsh in the national press, stressing that 'there will be further and faster growth than Palatine can ever achieve on its own'. They are still trying to persuade you that Palatine really needs Anglo-Welsh, and they are evidently prepared to spend vast amounts of *their* shareholders' money on national advertising to impress you.

The fact is, however, that it is Anglo-Welsh which needs Palatine, to improve its position in the on-trade sector. They want our tied estate and 'English heritage' beers to enable them to compete with the five major national tied estate brewers. That is no concern of yours: you *already own* the assets which Anglo-Welsh want so much.

Anglo-Welsh claim that their offer is 'extremely generous'. However, they know that your Company is not a lame duck, but widely described as one of the best managed in the industry. They are perfectly well aware that we have a unique portfolio for profitable growth: a portfolio of opportunities carefully and successfully identified by Palatine's own management over the past two years.

What they are trying to buy are assets which can best be developed by Palatine itself, including some which can *only* be developed by Palatine as an independent brewery.

Your Board and its financial advisers Purchase and Szell continue to recommend strongly that you reject the bid. In summary:

- Do not sell your shares.

- Do not accept Anglo-Welsh's offer.

- Keep your investment in a quality regional brewer.

- Keep Palatine independent.

Yours sincerely

(Signed) John Watson

PALATINE ALES PLC

Directors:	Registered Office:
J. Watson, M. Lester, T. Watson,	The Brewery
G. Phillips, D. Jones, F. Cox, L. Thomas	St Helens
	2 December 1985

Dear Shareholder,

It is with the greatest possible pleasure that I write to you once more, this time to confirm that your Company's independence has been preserved after a battle which has lasted over nine months.

Naturally I am addressing this letter particularly to those of you – the majority – who resisted all temptations and 'pressure selling' techniques to which you were exposed, and *stayed with us*!

To those who did agree to sell, but now find their acceptance forms are being returned to them, I can only hope that you are not too disappointed at being involuntarily back on the winning side!

We were tremendously encouraged by the active support we received throughout the battle from so many customers and employees, and a comfortable majority of your fellow shareholders have now demonstrated their confidence in our future, for Anglo-Welsh were only offered a further 6.7 per cent of shares to add to the 29.75 per cent they already owned.

Your Board and employees at all levels send you our very best wishes for a prosperous future with Palatine.

Yours sincerely

(Signed) John Watson

PART III: THE AFTERMATH

The Palatine Board met on Wednesday 4 December 1985. Fred Cox and Les Thomas sent their apologies. Most of the others were suffering from a degree of nervous exhaustion after the long takeover struggle. Nevertheless, it was necessary to think about the future. The discussion was initiated by the Chairman.

JOHN WATSON: Well, we've managed to see Anglo-Welsh off. I understand that they got 36.5 per cent of the total shareholding in the end, but Purchase and Szell say that they'll be unloading some of those and that they'll probably end up with about 20 per cent. Obviously that constitutes a threat for the future. What can we do to counter it?

DAN JONES: What about putting ourselves under somebody else's protection?

JOHN WATSON: It's possible. I've already had a couple of tentative enquiries. However, I don't see the point of fighting off one set of advances only to capitulate to the next. We got into this fight because we wanted to preserve our independence, and I don't think our views have changed, have they?

TOM WATSON: Mine haven't.

DAN JONES: Nor mine.

MIKE LESTER: I agree. But can't *we* expand? After all, that's how we got to be where we are now.

JOHN WATSON: I'd like to, but it's difficult. There aren't all that many small brewers left in the region, after all, and most of them already have formal or informal alliances of their own. As you know, I've been on the look out for some years for a smaller company we could have a friendly merger with, but there's nothing even remotely promising at the moment.

MIKE LESTER: Well, you know that scene better than anyone, so if you say it's not on we'll have to accept it. We'll have to try something else. I think our problem is that we're too closely identified with beer, and traditional draught beer at that. Everyone knows it's a stagnant market. We're vulnerable to another takeover bid, especially if there's another recession. I think we need to diversify.

GEORGE PHILLIPS: Funny you should say that. I was going to say the same thing.

JOHN WATSON: Have you something in mind?

GEORGE PHILLIPS: Yes, I have as a matter of fact. I was chatting the other week to a chap called Peter Davenport. He's the Managing Director and major shareholder in Acorn Hotels.

DAN JONES: I know them. They're one of our free trade accounts. They've got the Royal Oak at Knutsford and two or three other establishments in Cheshire and Lancashire.

GEORGE PHILLIPS: That's right. Well, Peter's getting close to retirement, and he was hinting that he'd like to sell out. I think there's a case for considering purchase. Acorn would provide us with a ready-made hotel chain ripe for further expansion. It's a logical move for us. Lots of brewers have moved into hotels, after all.

TOM WATSON: (*Doubtfully*) Well, I know the nationals have . . .

GEORGE PHILLIPS: And some regionals, too.

MIKE LESTER: (*Breaking in*) That's all very well, but I've another proposal entirely. I've been having discussions too, only in my case they've been with the Hughes family who run Cheshire Restaurants.

DAN JONES: Ah, yes, they're another of our free trade accounts. They're a chain with branches in places like Northwich, Wilmslow and Lymm . . .

MIKE LESTER: That's right. The thing is, they're likely to come on the market quite soon. Old Mr David Hughes has just been told by his doctors that he'll have to retire, and the younger members of the family would prefer to sell out and start up on their own. Like Acorn, it's a ready-made chain just ripe for expansion. I think it's where we ought to be going.

GEORGE PHILIPS: ⎫ (*Together*) Yes, but . . . Well I think . . .
TOM WATSON: ⎭

JOHN WATSON: Order, order, please gentlemen! We can't achieve much without more information. Let's meet again in a couple of weeks or so. George, perhaps you could let us have details of Acorn Hotels, and Mike, you do the same for Cheshire Restaurants . . . All right? Good. We'll consider your proposals fully then . . .

INSTRUCTIONS

As Personal Assistant to John Watson, prepare a report reviewing Palatine Ales' position following the successful conclusion of the takeover battle, evaluating the proposals made at the last Board meeting, and submitting your recommendations regarding future policy. You have at your disposal all the information on Palatine Ales contained in the last two cases, together with the earlier material on Acorn Hotels Ltd and Cheshire Restaurants Ltd.

SUGGESTIONS

Your answer might usefully include:

- An analysis of Palatine's strategic position in terms of threats, opportunities, strengths and weaknesses

- A consideration of Palatine's strategic options, using appropriate concepts and techniques

- A comparative evaluation of Acorn Hotels and Cheshire Restaurants as potential acquisitions, coupled with a recommendation as to which proposal (if either) should be adopted

- An assessment of any potential acquisition's current value and recommendations as to the offer price and acquisition strategy to be employed

- Capital financing and budgeting proposals relating to the above

- A consideration of the management implications of any proposed acquisition, including company reorganization and/or restructuring

- A supplementary Chairman's Statement incorporating financial forecasts and projections and issued with a view to deterring further takeover attempts.

ANSWERS

INTRODUCTION

We have included 'answers' to the three introductory cases in order to give you an idea of what we would be looking for if we were marking your responses. They are not intended to be narrowly restrictive, 'only-possible' solutions: instead, you should find that they suggest what kinds of factors you ought to be identifying in your analysis, and the range of possible solutions we think are sensible.

Assessing a case study answer is a two-stage process. The first stage consists of looking at how you have analysed the problem. This is relatively straightforward, because it is fairly easy to see whether you have identified the various factors involved reasonably correctly. If a case clearly invites you to redesign a kitchen because the existing layout doesn't conform to the food hygiene regulations and you miss this, then obviously you shouldn't get as many marks as someone who has spotted it. We once set a case involving a highly seasonal business which ended up with no cash, a big overdraft, lots of creditors and no hope of any more revenue for at least six months: those students who didn't recognize that some pretty drastic immediate action was required (surprisingly, there were several) couldn't reasonably expect any marks!

The second stage is the evaluation of your proposed solution. This is much more difficult, because one of the most important characteristics of case studies is that there isn't necessarily only one right answer. It is important that you should understand why this is so. The point is that nobody can be sure what the correct answer actually *is*. Even if the case is founded on a real-life situation, we only know what happened when the organization tried *one* solution. We can't know what would have happened if it had tried something else, nor (and this is important) what would have happened if someone else had tried the original solution. Managers have different talents and abilities, and what may work for one may not work for another. This means that your solution may differ, quite legitimately, from your neighbour's (in fact it is one of the characteristics of a good case study that it can give rise to equally valid alternative solutions).

This said, it is still possible to assess proposed solutions on a common-sense basis. A vague statement to the effect that you would 'call the staff together and get them to sell more effectively' doesn't carry much conviction, whereas an outline staff training programme coupled with precise incentives suggests that you know what you are doing, and is a great deal more persuasive. Perhaps 'persuasive' is the best note to end on: if you end up being able to write a report which analyses the problem convincingly and persuades your superiors to let you try to solve it your way, then our objective will have been achieved!

THE DUBBINGTONS CASE

As we said in the introduction, your response to this case can be organized in terms of the classic problem-solving structure. This also provides a useful framework for a report-style presentation. This is bound to be somewhat artificial, since the obligation to show *all* the stages of your reasoning forces you to appear rather more introspective than you would be in real life, but it still provides good practice in arranging and presenting material in an acceptable style. It might go along the following lines:

To: General Manager, Dubbingtons

From: P. Abbott and J. Shepherd,
         Joint Catering Managers, Dubbingtons

Date: Today's date

Subject: *Report on Disciplinary Incident*[1] (see notes on p. 13)

1. Facts
On Saturday afternoon store security officers stopped Chrissie____
___, a waitress, as she was leaving, searched her bags and found 11 lb of sliced ham and half-a-dozen eggs in them. Chrissie admitted that these came from the store restaurant's stocks, but claimed that she was given them by Fred_____, the chef, in return for her helping out over her lunch break in the kitchen, which was short-handed. Interviewed, Fred denied her story emphatically, pointing out that he had no authority to make that sort of deal.

As the management will be aware, Fred has been employed at

Dubbingtons for the past twelve years. He is well liked by the other departmental staff and undeniably possessed of excellent craft skills. However, the catering department has been suffering from higher-than-average food costs and labour turnover rates for several years now, though the available records do not disclose any obvious reasons for these. In consequence, the Board has recently created the post of Catering Manager to control this side of its operations, and we have been appointed.

We have only been in post for three weeks, but this is our second confrontation with Fred. The first was over the Board's decision to close the senior staff dining room. Fred apparently thinks we initiated this policy, and resents the fact that he will no longer be able to produce a certain number of high-quality meals.

The paucity of the records makes further investigation difficult. The catering staff are non-committal, and it seems very unlikely that they will be prepared to 'tell tales' against either Chrissie or Fred.[2]

2. Assumptions

It is not immediately clear whether or not Chrissie is telling the truth. If she is, then the problem of the higher-than-average food costs would appear to be explained, assuming that the practice she describes has been common. If she is lying, then we still have to find some other explanation. Chrissie is relatively young and inexperienced, and while she *may* be a hardened liar and criminal, we feel the balance of the probabilities is that she *is* telling the truth. This clearly implicates Fred. However, the facts still fit two alternative scenarios:

(a) Fred has been encouraging pilferage over a long period. Not only have food costs been above average, but the labour turnover has been relatively high, which is a little odd since Fred is generally considered to be genial and well liked (though we must add that we have found no evidence that this is true as far as his staff are concerned). Many people do not like working in an atmosphere of petty theft, and while they may not actually inform on their colleagues, they might well have taken the first opportunity to leave. This point helps to explain why there do not appear to have been many actual dismissals for pilferage (we assume that we would have been told if there had been an abnormally high incidence of these[3]), but we would still have expected there to be some if pilferage

199

has been common, particularly since store security is not under Fred's control.[4] The fact that there have not leads us to consider a possible alternative explanation.

(b) Food costs have been high in the past because Fred has not been as efficient as he might have been (he certainly seems to have neglected his record-keeping!), and his action in letting Chrissie take the food was motivated by his resentment at being demoted. This explanation fits the facts and is psychologically plausible.

Either explanation is reasonable, but the essential point is that both clearly point to poor control.[5]

3. Problems
We have divided these into two groups:

(a) *Short term:*
- What to do about Chrissie?
- What to do about Fred?

(b) *Long term:*
- What to do about control (this covers both pilferage and inefficient production methods)?
- What to do about the high labour turnover?
- Finally, how can we establish our authority over this department?[6]

4. Alternative Courses of Action
(a) *Do nothing.* Fairly obviously, this is not one of those situations where this is an acceptable solution. Doing nothing solves none of our problems and, by encouraging Fred, is likely to make most of them worse.[7]

(b) *Prosecution and/or dismissal.* It is dangerous to simplify law, but our understanding is that to convict someone of a serious crime like theft, we normally have to prove not only that they committed the alleged act, but also that they knew it was wrong. Chrissie cannot deny that she took the items, but she might well argue that she thought Fred had the authority to let her have them, and unless we can show that she had been told otherwise our prosecution might well fail, especially since the law traditionally recognizes that 'perks' are a feature of the catering industry. As for Fred, we have to remember that it is Chrissie's word against his, and that he is entitled to the benefit of any doubt. So it is unlikely that we could successfully prosecute either of them, even if we were willing to accept the expense and loss of time involved.

The same arguments apply to termination. Fred is protected against unfair dismissal, and in the absence of any previous official (i.e. provable) warnings he is likely to win in the event of an appeal. Chrissie is not protected to the same extent because she has not worked for long enough, and there *may* be grounds for dismissal.[8]

Let us assume for a moment that we could indeed fire her: should we? We have to consider staff attitudes and morale. On the one hand, they may think it unfair if we dismiss Chrissie and retain Fred. On the other, a dismissal would show that we were in earnest about stopping pilferage. The arguments would appear to be evenly balanced, but we must also consider whether Chrissie and Fred are likely to work well together in the future after she has 'informed' on him.

In our view, this tips the scales against Chrissie, though we recognize that there is room for argument here.[9]

(c) *Set up a proper control system*. Neither prosecution nor dismissal really solves the underlying problems, and our emphasis must be on establishing control. This must include a proper system of recording orders, stocks, issues, consumption and wastage.[10] It should also include issuing a statement of policy regarding 'perks', to form part of all present and future contracts of employment,[11] together with an intensified programme of random checks to show that we really mean what we say. What this does is:

- It helps to solve our problems with Chrissie and Fred by making it clear that we are doing something about the food costs.

- It should lead to a reduction in the food costs themselves.

- It *may* help to improve the labour turnover figures by improving morale, though this is not certain. We would recommend additional measures such as termination of employment interviews in order to establish the real reasons for the increase.

- It establishes our authority as catering managers, since we are shown to be not only in charge but doing something positive.

5. Recommendations

Fairly obviously, it is Alternative 4(c) which points the way forward. We would couple this with an investigation to discover the real cause or causes of the high labour turnover (which may turn out to have nothing to do with the immediate problem). We would also suggest an attempt to conciliate Fred by returning the responsibility for special functions to him. After all, he is competent and well liked, and we should try to retain him if possible. If he accepts the new system, well and good. If he does not, then it is up to *him* to resign, which avoids any problems with unfair dismissal and allows us to recruit a new chef who will start with a clear idea of his position and responsibilities.

Notes

1. This uses the 'memo heading' format we mentioned earlier. There is no need to invent imaginary names: in fact, if you were doing this report as an assignment, you could put your tutor's name opposite the 'To'.

2. This kind of summary is possible with a relatively short case, but you will find that it becomes progressively more difficult with the longer ones. In fact, it doesn't earn many marks, if any, and you should reduce it to the minimum. We have included it here because it is required by the context (i.e. a disciplinary report).

3. This gets round the case's failure to provide some important background facts. Most cases have this kind of 'hole' in them, and it is useful to be able to circumvent them smoothly.

4. A common-sense assumption, so obvious as not to need labelling as such. Practically all stores reserve the right to search employees and their baggage as a matter of course.

5. This is by far the most important conclusion you can come to in this section. The temptation is to concentrate on trying to find some way of proving Fred's guilt or innocence. In fact, the real point is to get this department functioning efficiently.

6. This is probably too introspective (i.e. self-critical) to be

included in a real-life report, but it is a genuine problem none the less, and you need to show that you have recognized it as such.

7. Again, this is a little too 'introspective' for inclusion in a real-life report. At this stage, however, you are only *practising* decision-making, and it is useful to set out all the stages of your thinking. Common sense should tell you what is likely to strike an employer as unduly negative.

8. These two paragraphs provide a fairly bald summary of the legal position. They could be 'enriched' by references to the statutes involved and possible precedents. However, don't get carried away to the extent of seeing this as a purely legal problem. The real point is still control.

9. You will see that we have followed our own advice and climbed down off the fence here. As markers, we would be happy enough to see you argue either way as long as you recognized that there is indeed room for argument over this point.

10. These ought to be set out in much more detail in a complete answer. The necessary measures are obvious enough, and you should be familiar with them from your work on food and beverage control.

11. You might draft a specimen statement and show it as an appendix. This would certainly 'enrich' your answer. Remember that one of the things we are looking for is the ability to *implement* solutions.

THE HARDY HALL CASE

As we have said, you don't have to stick to the classic problem-solving structure in detail when laying out your response. In fact, you shouldn't in this instance, because the case itself asks for an answer divided into two main sections.

1. Operational Implications

This is relatively simple, because it is simply a question of working out whether, and if so how, you can accommodate the two conferences.

(a) *Cleaning.* Obviously, you will have to allow for cleaning after the students depart on March 28. The question to be asked is whether your 4 cleaners can clean 30 rooms in 5 hours at 45 minutes per room. If not, you will have either to see whether they could start earlier on some rooms, recruit another cleaner from somewhere or else help out yourself. Your answer to this will affect your costings. The same problem will crop up again after the first conference, though less acutely since the cleaning times are reduced. You ought also to allow for weekend cleaning (how many cleaners will you need?), which may be difficult since the case says that the staff are married women with their own family commitments.

(b) *Laundry.* Students provide their own linen, but the Hall presumably maintains a stock of blankets, etc. The sheet, pillow-case and towel calculations are fairly simple once you have decided how many to allocate to each conference guest and how often they are to be replaced.

(c) *Food.* Both conferences will require breakfasts, lunches and dinners, weekends included, and your staff (even the full-time ones) only work Mondays to Fridays, so you will have to allow for overtime. Your catering assistants normally do split shifts, which won't cover the lunches, so you will have to cover these with extra hours. The other important question is the nature of the meals provided, because this will affect the food cost. It seems unlikely that the breakfasts will alter much, but you will have to judge what would be acceptable for the two conferences (we think that the evening meal ought to be a three course affair with a food cost closer to £2 or so).

2. Conference Pricing

It looks as though you can accommodate both conferences, but what price should you charge? Before looking at the two conferences under consideration, it is useful to construct an outline income and expenditure account, which might look something like this:

Hardy Hall: Income and Expenditure Account

	£	£	£
Income			39,690
Food costs:			
Breakfasts		4,306	

	£	£	£
Dinners	7,045		
Wages:			
Cook	6,150		
Assistant cook	5,250		
Catering assistants	5,883	28,634	
Accommodation costs:			
Cleaners	6,986		
Laundry	—	6,986	35,620
Overheads:			2,606
Bursar	9,900		
Porter	4,144		
Rates	2,500		
Water	500		
Light and heat	2,400		
Repairs etc.	2,350		
Telephone	400		
Sundries	250		22,444
Excess of expenditure over income			£(19,838)

Don't worry if your figures differ a little in detail. Some of them involve assumptions, and a difference of plus or minus 5 per cent isn't really significant.

Note that we have distinguished between 'direct' and 'overhead' costs. Doing so reveals that total revenue is very close to the total of the direct costs. This is probably more than just coincidence: it suggests that the Hall's financial policy has been to cover the direct costs and subsidize the overheads.

Now to the detailed calculations. You will already have considered most of the factors under 'operational implications', but don't forget that you need to allow for the tea, coffee and biscuits that the second conference will be consuming in substantial quantities. You should also consider those sherry receptions, which almost certainly constitute a 'sale' of intoxicating liquor to the delegates. You might be able to obtain an occasional permission, but if you are going to do this frequently you will require an occasional licence (if you do, the licensee would presumably provide the sherry). Finally, the allocation of the overheads raises some tricky questions. Strictly speaking, most of these are fixed costs (i.e. they will be incurred whether you host the conferences or not). However, items like lighting, heating and telephone will probably show an increase, and you should perhaps build in some kind of an allowance. We suggest that you might work out a daily rate for lighting, repairs, telephone and sundries (on the basis of a 36 week year) and then charge that.

Ignoring the licence problem and the various trips and entertainments (which we think will be the responsibility of the conference organizers), your cost calculations may well come to something like the following. Again, don't worry if you get slightly different results, as your assumptions may differ from ours (for instance, we have assumed two sheets, two pillowcases and two towels per guest, changed once for the longer of the two conferences).

	Conference No. 1 £	£	Conference No. 2 £	£
Cleaning:				
Rooms: Daily	88		53	
End	24		24	
Public areas	30	142	16	93
Laundry		108		54
Food:				
Breakfasts	231		66	
Lunches	270		90	
Dinners	420		120	
Sundries			60	
Wages: Cook	201		106	
Assistant cook	149		79	
Catering assistants	360	1,631	254	775
Overheads		150		. 64
Totals		£2,031		£986
Average per head		68		30

So what price should you charge? Simply to cover your direct costs would be ridiculous, because you need to try to make something to cover the other overheads such as bursar's and porter's salaries, rates and water rates, and you want a profit as well. As far as the food is concerned, you might consider some formula based on costs since this is widely understood and accepted. Because the service standards are likely to be somewhat lower than in a commercial operation, you might set the rate so that they were 50 per cent (or even 60 per cent) of the total. The same point applies to the accommodation. After all, the bathroom and toilet provision (one of each per floor) is hardly luxurious, and you don't have a bar, so some of the participants are going to feel that the surroundings are a bit on the spartan side. This is where you really need that information about the competition. Some formula such as 50 per cent of the current local room rate (given the place and period this might be about £30) might be acceptable. Your calculations might then end up looking something like this:

	Conference No. 1		Conference No. 2	
	£	£	£	£
Proposed charges:				
Food (per head)	51		19	
Rooms (per head)	105	156	45	64
Totals		4,685		1,910
Profit		2,654		924

If you could make a profit of approximately £2,500 per week for the fourteen or so unoccupied weeks (a big if!) you would turn that excess of expenditure over income into an income surplus.

There are of course some longer-term implications. Perhaps you ought to reconsider the bathroom and toilet provision, which will require expensive structural alterations and affect your pricing proposals. You should also consider whether you need a licence, and if so, what the structural and staffing implications will be. Certainly the staff terms and conditions of service need to be renegotiated. Of course, improving the facilities ought to allow you to charge higher prices.

THE CASE OF GEORGE AND MARIE

Once again, you have a case which asks for an answer divided into two main sections, which means that you can't use the classic problem-solving structure.

1. Analysis

Introduction
L'Auberge has been successful in the past because:

(a) It maintained high standards in the past since George and Marie insisted on these and were able to work together to achieve them.

(b) It did so without incurring high costs because:

- The purchasing was efficient.

- Labour was local, turnover was low and staff relations were good.

- The management overhead was low, since the restaurant was run by the owners with only relatively junior supervisors.

The challenge was to expand L'Auberge without (a) sacrificing standards or (b) raising costs unacceptably. The operating statements suggest that this has not been done.

Problems
These are clearly centred on the figures revealed by the operating statements, and these provide a convenient framework for considering them.

(a) *Sales*. There is no evidence of any feasibility study having been carried out. It appears that the Brasserie was opened on the basis of a 'hunch', and while it may well have a ready-made market in L'Auberge's existing clientele, there was always a risk that this would simply be split between the two units. The case says nothing about other restaurants, but there are almost bound to be more in a city centre location. Competition from established businesses can be formidable. Note, however, that while this may help to explain why the Brasserie's sales are disappointing, it doesn't really explain why L'Auberge's have fallen.

What about prices? If you have carried out the calculations suggested, you will have found that average spend per head in 1983 was roughly £9.00, in 1984 £10.50 and in 1985 £11.75. Either customers have been choosing more expensive menu and wine list items or (much more likely) prices have been increasing. If the latter, why? The note indicates that the rate of increase is higher than that for restaurant prices in general over this period, and this could account for some of the reduction in business. To decide whether or not the increases are realistic, you have to look at the expenses side.

(b) *Cost of sales.* It is easy enough to calculate this as a percentage of sales and to show that costs have gone up not only absolutely but relatively. They have also gone up faster than the national figures. The increase is slightly less in the case of beverages, which is what one would expect given that wine stocks could service two establishments more easily than food ones. The really worrying thing is that Marie is said to have obtained improved terms from suppliers (understandable, given that she is ordering larger quantities). If this is the case, why are the food cost percentages higher? You should clearly be thinking about weaknesses in control: wastage, perhaps, or even pilferage.

(c) *Labour cost.* You will have noted that this has more than doubled between 1983 and 1984, and increased again in 1985. This is only to be expected, since the Brasserie has been set up along similar lines to L'Auberge (i.e. it has the same staff). Actually, it is rather surprising that the labour cost hasn't gone up more, especially in view of the national rates. Quite apart from the inevitable pay rises, you would expect the Brasserie's wages to be a bit up on L'Auberge's since city centre rates are likely to be higher. You will have noted the additional appointment of at least one wine waiter: the fact that the total wages bill hasn't increased by more than about 2.2 per cent suggests that there have been some compensating reductions, probably in the part-time staff, and almost certainly in view of the decline in trade.

There is also the question of the increase in labour turnover: this is bound to have increased costs to some extent. You could attribute this labour turnover problem in part to George's inevitable absences. You might be tempted to attribute it to lowish wage rates (at the Brasserie?), but a good answer would produce figures to justify this assertion (you know both the staffing structure and the total wage bill for 1983, at least, so you could work out the average gross wage per annum and relate it to what you knew about catering wages for the period). What the figures don't show is the effect

209

of the overall increase in labour turnover on standards: it can't have been good, and this helps account for some of the loss of business.

(d) *Overhead cost.* This has gone up in virtually the same proportion as the labour cost. Again, it isn't unexpected. After all, there is loan interest to take into account, not to mention city centre rates, rent (George and Marie won't have *bought* a city centre property for the £60,000 mentioned in the case) and the increased travelling expenses. As with labour costs, the surprising thing is that the total overheads haven't increased by more. So what have George and Marie been skimping on? Well, one pretty glaring omission in the case is any mention of marketing and promotion. L'Auberge was built up slowly, probably to a large extent by word of mouth. The Brasserie was launched as a fully fledged operation expected to do the same level of business as L'Auberge from the start. It needed a substantial amount of advertising, and the figures suggest that it didn't get it.

2. Recommendations

Fairly obviously, your recommendations should be aimed at correcting the weaknesses you have identified. The problems faced by George and Marie stem from their failure to plan, organize and control the expansion effectively.

As far as planning is concerned, there seems to have been a failure to examine the proposal realistically. There was no feasibility study and no proper marketing plan. Without these, you can't really tell whether or not it was a good idea to set up yet another restaurant in the city centre. There's no obvious reason why it shouldn't be successful, however, as long as standards can be maintained, costs controlled and enough cash be found to launch a much needed advertising campaign.

Organizationally, the weakness has been the failure to develop an appropriate management structure. At some stage in their development, expanding businesses have to change from omnipresent owner management to some form of delegated authority. George and Marie simply can't be present at both establishments all the time: they have to appoint unit managers, set them clear targets and perhaps adopt more 'functional' roles themselves. You need to explore the cost implications of this. George and Marie clearly need to do some manpower planning, starting with themselves: Marie could clearly do with a bit of training in delegation, and George might benefit from a course in marketing.

This is linked with a failure to develop an appropriate system of operational and management control. It is probably this which accounts for the menu price rises. Setting prices in relation to costs is all right as long as the latter are under control, but here they clearly aren't: it is obvious that if Marie's back is turned, food either gets wasted or goes missing. Checking the takings late at night is no substitute for a proper budgetary control system. This needs to be spelled out in some detail.

All this should be obvious enough, but your real problem is to suggest how George and Marie can finance the changes needed, which will take time to become effective. One useful trick is to put yourself in the position of their bank manager and ask what conditions you would impose before lending them any more money. You would certainly need convincing that they were going to change their management practices.

You might also consider whether they ought to continue with their attempt to run a second restaurant at all. Possibly the Brasserie could be sold and most of the investment recovered for use elsewhere. If they still wanted to expand their original business there are other ways of doing so: there might be scope for a small hotel at L'Auberge, for instance, or for outside catering around Chelmslow, or they might even capitalize on George's knowledge of French wines by setting up an off-licence and specialist wine importation business. These are strategic alternatives which would capitalize on George and Marie's strengths and minimize their weaknesses: it is the business of a case study answer to identify these alternatives and not just to assume that the proprietors have to go on as they started.

INDEX